M.P.E. Lennon

I0144882

The Next 2000 Days

God & Man in Obama Two

Why he will win
Why you'll regret it.

ISBN: 0984836705
ISBN-13: 9780984836703
Library of Congress Control Number: 2012938492
Bach University Press, Chicago, IL

to Linna, Sandra, Dana, mothers of beautiful children;
and to Jessie without whom this book would never have been
written.

Outline of Chapters

Introduction

This is a book about the future. Not some far off, distant future of generations hence, but your future, a future as intense and tumultuous as the rise of Fascism and Communism in the last century. And it's right at your doorstep.

Admit it. As soon as you read the above paragraph, you started to feel an interest, however slight, perhaps even thinking, "Could it be true?" Such is the nature of our reaction to predictions.

Predictions are an inescapable part of our life. Maybe they are, in a sense, the forbidden fruit. Who can know the future for certain? Some of us would say only the Divine may and He grudgingly doles it out to far too few prophets over the ages. But not to predict at all may be irresponsible. We have been given the gifts of prudence and wisdom, and it just wouldn't do to find the cupboard bare someday down the road when there is something we can do right now to prevent that from happening in the future.

Then, too, we get a certain joy out of predicting things, savoring an outcome before it arrives.

A student thinks, "I'm graduating in just four months."

A pregnant mom says, "The baby's due in August."

And a whole lot of us chant to ourselves, "I get off work in two hours."

And sometimes we even hope for a less favorable outcome: "Just wait. He'll get his. Just wait."

But there are those other things in the future that we really want to know about. Who will win the presidential election in 2012? What will happen to the economy? This book will give you an answer, a clear, unambivalent, reasoned answer. What kind of a book does that?

Let's say we wanted to take all the predictions that are made on a daily basis and categorize them. We might come up with something like this:

1. Mom-and-pop predictions

2. Hubristic forecasts

3. Professional futuring.

The anticipation of graduation, the expectant mother, and so on—these fall into the first category: mom-and-pop predictions, events in our future that we kind of have to think about to make it through life.

But if you're the type that considers yourself an expert on some topic, loves to get your face on TV, and looks forward to being quoted in newspapers, then you are clearly the second type, the hubristic forecaster. But be warned: hubristic experts get the most seething criticism of all predictors. UC Berkeley's business school professor Philip Tetlock asserts that "the better known and more frequently quoted they are, the less reliable their guesses about the future are likely to be."

The third category is the type of forecast attempted in the pages of this book. Like mom-and-poppers, professional futurists predict as a necessity. A business needs to forecast funds available to pay workers; an organization needs to know how the health and tax reform regulations will affect it over the next five years. Professional futuring calls on technology and concepts from a large number of fields of study that assist, but in no way limit, the intuition.

But how likely is it that even professional futurists can really, well, see the future?

Consider this: you are at some spot right this instant—standing, sitting, or reclining. Imagine yourself at that very same spot some ten or twenty years ago. What was it like back then?

Twenty years ago

Take a look about you in that past. Think of all the complexities in your own life and in the lives of the people about you. Look at what is happening in business, in the industrial and technological developments that are just starting to take place at this time. What is happening politically? Culturally?

Now consider that looking into the future from that point (to your true present) all those changes have to evolve from what you see in your imagination to what surrounds you at this very moment. As difficult as it may seem to figure out the path, the evidence is there in front of you, the path to where you are today.

Back to the present

Now look forward twenty years into the future. Isn't it the same thing? Difficult as it may be to ferret it out, whatever comes about must develop from what is around you. If you can envision it, almost feel it, then you have some idea of what it is that excites futurists.

Tools of futuring—the scenario

A scenario is one of the tools of modern futuring that helps us imagine this path, to add flesh to a storyline that takes us from the present to the future. It's like a screenplay with real characters (like Obama, Pelosi, Boehner, Romney) and events (like elections and the aftermath). Consider that, by means of a scenario, you may actually be looking at what is to come—at a detailed view of the future.

How do you create such a scenario? It might start in a rather simple way—just toss up on the board some names and ideas:

- Van Jones

- Obama's statement on the economy

- Holder's legal action as attorney general

To these initial conditions you add and connect data with future events, events already scheduled, and decision time points that appear inevitable. You ask, "What if?" and explore consequences at every level of society. In the end, it is really difficult to create all that complex interactive activity underpinning the political, economic, and social phenomena for the period—often too difficult to form a trustworthy analysis. But, every now and then, the exception occurs—a scenario that is so compelling, so convincing and internally consistent, so profound, that it requires your attention. I believe *The Next 2000 Days*, the story that begins right before the presidential election of 2012, is just that kind of a scenario.

PART ONE

Some things about futuring.

CHAPTER 1.

Uncertainty & Subjectivity

Uncertainty and subjectivity are two things that must be taken into consideration with any scenario.

First: Uncertainty.

In the 1970s, real estate company ads were plentiful. Nearly every night there was Century 21 on the TV with the happy faces and catchy jingles. "Buy land," was a common saying, "because they ain't making any more." It seemed logical enough.

Real estate prices climbed. Back in 2001 you might have noticed this trend and predicted that from 2001 to 2006 the price of homes would increase. You would have been right. You would have successfully predicted the future based on a trend.

> **Trend**—*prolonged period of time when prices in a financial market are rising or falling faster than their historical average.*

Whenever we see a trend we should ask, "What are the conditions supporting this trend?" In the case of real estate values, the assumption of continuing demand was the trend support. (Not making land any more, remember?) But there was another assumption that most people neglected: that there would always be money to pay for those homes. In other words, as homes became more expensive, buyers would be making enough money with their increased earnings to pay for those new valuations of real estate. Income would rise along with housing prices.

Didn't happen.

The higher priced homes were bought through increased borrowing rather than bigger paychecks. Americans therefore developed another trend—widespread borrowing. The nation saw a debt-to-income ratio rise from 75 percent in 1990 to 130 percent in 2010. The higher value of homes put them well out of the reach of the average family. Without buyers for all that real estate, valuation dropped. The trend was gone. Suddenly, the bubble burst.

Moreover the plummeting price of homes affected personal and household wealth. Almost 16.4 trillion evaporated from investment portfolios and retirement savings.

Working with trends and bubbles

It's the job of the scenario creator to watch for bubbles. Trends help in forecasting, but the future is made up of both trends and uncertainties about the continuance of such trends.

TRENDS IN THE UNITED STATES

The **dollar** fell steadily throughout 2010 to the third quarter of 2011; it dropped 21 percent in 2010 alone.

Gold was $300 an ounce in 2002 and soared to its present high of well over $1500.

The national debt was 14 trillion in 2011, having risen from 3 trillion in 1990. The debt actually rose by 3.7 trillion since Obama took office.

Even more difficult to predict are events that have a very low probability of occurring but can nevertheless have a significant impact on the entire scenario.

EXAMPLES OF HIGH IMPACT, LOW PROBABILITY EVENTS

Nuclear attack on the United States.

Obama doesn't run (e.g. is not nominated by Democratic Party).

Half the justices of the Supreme Court fall fatally ill.

It's interesting to note how helpful well-crafted scenarios can actually work. A financial industries scenario had called for the establishing of alternative trading locations for the financial markets in New York in the event of future disasters. This allowed them to continue to function right after a high impact/low probability event— **the 9/11 attack on the ongoing site in the World Trade Center.**

Allowing for subjectivity

> *"The battle to feed all of humanity is over. In the 1970s hundreds of millions of people will starve to death in spite of any crash programs embarked upon now. At this late date nothing can prevent a substantial increase in the world death rate."*

The above quote is from the 1968 publication *The Population Bomb,* written by Paul Ehrlich, a prime target of journalist Dan

Gardner's critical text: *Future Babble.* The subtitle, *Why Expert Predictions Are Next to Worthless, and You Can Do Better,* sort of says it all.

Ehrlich's Prediction (1960):	India, with a population of 400 million, will have widespread famine.
Fact: (2012):	India, with a population of 1.2 billion in 2010, has had no record of famine.
Amartya Sen:	(Nobel Prize
Economist):	"Nations with democracy and a free press have virtually never suffered from extended famines."

There is no mistaking Ehrlich for anything but a hubristic forecaster. Charles Rubin noted Ehrlich's "emotionally gripping style...he does not try to convince intellectually by mind dulling statistics...[but] roars like an old testament prophet." A member of British Parliament once noted that no word is so often used with the word "civilization" as the word "destruction." Ehrlich's appearances on celebrity talk shows such as the then popular *The Tonight Show Starring Johnny Carson,* as well as his appearances on dozens of college campuses validate his propensity for showmanship. Everywhere he went, he promoted the urgency of self-sterilization for young people. To those who completed the procedure, his team handed out an oversized button to wear announcing the "accomplishment." At the University of California in Berkeley was a standing joke: just get hold of a button and you could use it to encourage a reluctant female to have sex with you, falsely assuring her there was no risk of conceiving.

It's interesting to observe how Paul Ehrlich reacted to those who reminded him of his failed thesis because his reaction is typical of those who make widely-read but failed predictions. Writing in the *New Yorker,* Philip Teloch notes: "When they are wrong they are rarely held accountable and they rarely admit it either. They insist they were just off on timing." It's hardly a surprise then, that like many gloom and doom predictors, Ehrlich maintains that the problem still exists and the fatal events may yet occur.

A hubristic Ehrlich also suggests that widespread famine didn't happen because the world heeded his call and avoided the danger. This is an absurd statement; it was the development of technology and reasoning in solving needs of developing human problems that accounted for the increase in food supply.

> **Ehrlich's solution**—*the wholesale extinguishing of new human life. His call was that India should have their food aid eliminated because they were hopeless. (Would Ehrlich and company have eliminated the lives of over 800,000 Indians?)*

Since the claim that his solutions were adopted and famine thereby avoided doesn't let him off the hook, Ehrlich hides behind a remarkable statement: If you think he made predictions, you are all "idiots." He merely used UN population data and repeated predictions that others had made. Blame them. However, modern futurists take full responsibility for the selection of material they choose to use in their scenarios and do not blame others. **If they use it, they own it.**

Subjectivity: Ehrlich's undoing

Ehrlich, like all of us who undertake the task of futuring, must face the overwhelming tendency to fall prey to subjectivity.

All creators of scenarios must deal with this tendency.

What might be Ehrlich's source of subjectivity? Perhaps the ideological Ehrlich resents man as a slave to energy and other resources. Man appears to go about creating new life as it moves him without any regard for circumstances. And what is most poignant for Ehrlich (and many others) is that this procreative reaction takes its support from organized religion: "Be fruitful and multiply." This doctrinal mandate strikes Ehrlich as yet another conspiracy against the intellectual progress of human kind, i.e. science. Ehrlich's scenario marshals a resistance against this impulse; population growth is not merely an explosive phenomenon; *it's a "bomb"! It's deadly.*

Note that to solve the problem, Ehrlich does not merely recommend working to resolve the constraints on accommodating a population rise, but rather putting an end to the population expansion itself. Ehrlich didn't want to just solve the problem: he wanted to solve it in accordance with an ideology.

Creating the scenario: dealing with uncertainty and subjectivity

Looking at the problems of uncertainty and subjectivity one might ask how it is possible to effectively deal with these and still come up with a good scenario. However one creates a future scenario, it must measure up to standards of evaluation. Not all scenarios have the same value. To some, a scenario looks something like a screenplay, and in a way they are right. What makes a good scenario, however, is not the same thing that makes a good film script, though there are similarities in the requirements of logical consistency within the story. The quality of the scenario starts with an excellent research team that gathers and analyzes available data. Even with good data, though, intuition plays a role. A good scenario designer has a certain feel to how things will play out, given an antecedent situation.

When it's all done, the creator of a scenario must ask, "Can I defend it? What is its plausibility? Is it logically consistent in its elements and the environment in which it will play out? " You should ask the same questions about the scenario I'll present in the pages that follow. This scenario is created in a time of historical, political, and financial instability. How subjective is it? How strong are the arguments?

Any given scenario may be cross-referenced with other scenarios prepared by independent parties, but the true test of its validity is, of course, the future.

How our scenario differs from professional scenarios

There are, however, some ways in which the scenario presented in *The Next 2000 Days* differs from those offered by professional planners. Due to the nature of this work, we are offering a single scenario, whereas it is customary for futuring consultants to prepare several. Furthermore, almost all scenarios require some degree of modification. Scenarios change as new information becomes available. Since updating for new information is not possible here, I have, at various points in the scenario, suggested alternatives to what I believe are the most likely events. If the key events that occur are other than as stated, an alternative future is suggested.

CHAPTER 2.

Forces Controlling
the Future

It is said that the surest way to predict the future is to create it. But can man do that? Is the future simply a matter of man's will, or is there something that prevents us from creating the kind of world we want?

You've heard people say that there is a cycle, a certain pattern to history or even that history repeats itself. Some people feel that all of mankind's prior experience on this planet is directing him to a certain future point, to things like increased consciousness, liberty, and self-expression. All of this suggests the existence of a possible force at work in history and in creating the future.

The history of the last century records some pretty dramatic changes: the Russian Communist Revolution, the rise of Fascism, the creation of Maoist China. We are told we can trace this all back to a single short-statured, mild-mannered man who believed in forces at work in history—the philosopher Georg Wilhelm Friedrich Hegel. As philosopher historians Branowski and Mazlish note, "It is therefore remarkable that out of his (Hegel's) academic work should grow a way of looking at men and states which has overturned empires."

How is it that Hegel's philosophy did all that?

We can oversimplify here. (After all, this isn't a philosophy class.) Hegel said that when we see something new develop, it arises from an opposite antecedent. Take a look at what happens when you mix water and cement. One is a liquid, the other a powder. When you put them together what happens? You get something new—concrete.

The newness, according to Hegel, is good, but it comes about through the meeting of opposites, and therefore the potential for conflict exists; a struggle arises. Hegel, according to many, had a certain admiration for violence. His followers adapted such a notion to their own theses. For example, Darwin saw a contest for survival in his theory of evolution, Marx touted class warfare in his dialectical materialism. To quote Lenin, "You can't make an omelet without breaking a few eggs."

What about us today? We're on the verge of what is sure to be one of the most hotly contested presidential elections in history. What can Hegel's philosophy tell us about ourselves?

Much of Hegel's legacy has distilled down to us in our current political concepts. Hegel used the terms "thesis" to denote the existing entity, the thing that must be transformed, and "anti-thesis" to refer to its opposite. We use the terms "liberal" and "conservative" when speaking about political candidates. The goal of the liberal, now also called progressive, like the Hegelian anti-thesis, is to change society (the thesis), to move it on to an end reminiscent of utopia. The conservative, on the other hand (thesis), frequently finds himself defending things in the current state, i.e. "Don't you see? Utopia is here and now.".

Being on the right side of history

The liberals pride themselves on having the enlightened view of things, and, many times, the conservatives do appear clueless. Bronowski notes that "progressives have tended to claim that history marches on their side. Perhaps it is true of all progressive ideas that their adherents must feel themselves to be going with the stream of history. On the other hand, traditionalists have often seemed to believe that history has reached its climax in them."

This idea of being on the side of history has extraordinary appeal. Progressives claim they ally themselves with every advance in human society, with the victory of science and knowledge over disease and ignorance, with advancing humanity through civil rights legislation and militating against discrimination in every conceivable instance of human existence. This appeal is the second most important reason I maintain that, despite any polling numbers, Obama will win the next election. It is why actor Mogan Freeman could label the Tea Party adherents as racists even though their champion at the time, Herman Cain, was a black man. He's on the wrong side of history. It's not logical, but historical.

But, for all that, progressives have one big problem—the exquisite difficulty of defining and establishing the precise functioning of this end state they wish to create.

In his address to the Latin American Bishops in 1997, then Cardinal Josef Ratzinger noted that leftist regimes failed because "They tried to change the world without knowing what is good and what is not good for the world, without knowing in what direction the world must be changed in order to make it better."

What is lacking in progressives, then, is not action but rather a certain perennial truth. How do you change the world when what you actually seek is an unchanging truth?

Back to the question: Are there forces in history other than what man dictates?

Today, most professional futurists would take issue with the notion that history is guided to some ultimate end. They "see no immutable force in the flow of history, no invisible hands of predestination, fate or economic determinism." The rise and fall of political entities are determined by man's will or misconceptions. Hegel's philosophy is not a necessary sociobiological rule.

The result is just wish fulfillment. People want to change things and therefore take advantage of opportunities to do so. In short, Hegel just offered people a rationalization to do what they really wanted to do.

A different view of history

While it is true that history flows under no identifiable force but rather is created by men of free will, it is certainly possible that movement in history follows some principles. Let me explain this further.

First, a trip to the museum.

Guide in the Sistine Chapel, The Vatican, Italy

"The ceiling Sistine Chapel bears one of the most well-known and famous artworks of all time—the remarkable *The Creation of Adam* painted circa 1511 by Michelangelo. God's right arm is outstretched to impart life to a completely naked Adam. Adam's finger and God's finger are approaching each other-but are not together yet: a dramatization that conveys the gentleness of a touching."

Embryology Note

If we look at a developing human life, we come across a tiny structure that looks like a blackberry except it's not black; rather, it's pink and is even called a morula, which is Latin for mulberry. That's right: we all start our careers as humans as little berries.

But if we look at that berry in more detail, we notice that it is made up of a number of divisions. The single, fertilized egg that came from mom and dad putting together an egg and a sperm divides a dozen or so times, ending up as a morula.

Now, if we were to stop and make a scientific study of this dividing berry, we would come up with a grave finding: The structure is doomed. The cells will overpopulate and soon be deprived of surface area needed for diffusion of nutrients. Necrosis will ensue, turning the morula into nothing more than a heap of dead cells. How can one stop it? Stop the cells from dividing. (Sound familiar? Think of population biologists like Ehrlich.)

But as the morula reaches the thirty-two-cell stage, something marvelous happens. The cells come very close to each other. They form a tight relationship called **compaction**. They create a space and then there is a pushing in, like from the gentle force of some invisible finger. The structure that we claimed was doomed continues to survive, to gain access to nutrients, to become something greater than one could ever imagine from just looking at its past state.

It's possible Michelangelo, as a result of his intensive studies of human anatomy in the Monastery of Santo Spirito, became familiar with this observation of the embryo, and that his painting reflects life coming from such subtle forces rather than some spectacular spark.

Analysis

The changes in the embryo develop from structural antecedents. Its development follows an order not immediately apparent, but embryologists have identified some of these determinants.

Argument

Is it not also possible that history, the history of man past and his future, follows some such elusive but dependable principle? This may be similar to what is being proposed by contemporary theories of biological structuralism. Structualists do not deny evolution but suggest it follows orderly principles. A scenario such as the one I offer may reflect influences similar to the principles of biological structuralism. The changes in our history appear random and unpredictable as we encounter them, but there still may be some underlying principle governing them. That is the concept of history both past history and history in the making that we want to be open to in futuring.

PART TWO

Definition of Forces: The Starting Point

CHAPTER 3

Current Financial Outlook

When it comes to the subject of money, we're no strangers to predicting. We incessantly ask "How much is in my pocket? How much will be in my paycheck? How much will I spend this weekend? On and on it goes. For many it's a process done too late in the game and with too little skill to really control their future. Futuring in finance and economics can be helpful in exploring the likely results in the 2012 election and the following 2000 days.

Economics and our political behavior

Concern about our own situations makes us think about what's happening in the economic world about us. How does what's happening affect the dough in our pockets? We watch for announcements of an increase in taxes and follow the news on the job market. We know that layoff and hiring figures may eventually affect us or someone close to us if they haven't already.

By now everyone above the age of two realizes we're worming our way out of a recession. Ask how it came about and you usually get a lot of finger-pointing and complex answers including the following: minorities defaulted on risky loans that never should have been made, S&Ls engaged in predatory lending, greedy Wall Streeters took money for bad investments induced by a frenzy for profit in marketing of subprime-mortgage-backed lending, a decline occurred in easy money from world markets, oversight agencies failed to respond to whistle blowers. All have been mentioned.

But any reasonable analysis would have to conclude that the anemic economic situation resulted from complicated, long-developing problems, a failure in both earnings growth and credit supply. It was a perfect storm: everything came together to contribute to an impossible situation.

The sensible question to ask now is where are we headed? What is in store? Are things getting better or worse? Consider the following:

Peter Thiel is a man who wants to invest in private flights into space and villages under the sea. If you're thinking that this sounds a little too much like something from Jules Vernes or H.G. Wells, that's fine with him, but keep in mind he is a billion-dollar venture capitalist, was the first to invest in Facebook, and is a cofounder of PayPal. And yes, he wants to look at science fiction for business investment ideas.

Why would he want to do that?

If we look around at the current financial situation, it's no secret that we have enormous debt, which threatens to just keep on growing. But what is worse, as far as investors like Thiel are concerned, is that we have little prospect of income growth. As Wired's Gary Wolf reported, Thiel worries that nobody seems to realize that we need to make money and don't have a growth sector to accomplish that.

Some Definitions-

NICE: non-inflation, constant expansion.-what we had in the past.

DRAG: a period characterized by "an anemic growth outlook at a time of a push for deficit reduction." This is now.

How bad is it?

The gross domestic product (GDP) is a good indicator of how well a country is doing financially. It tallies up the total dollar value of all goods and services produced over a specific time period. You can think of it as the size of the economy, and it is usually expressed as a percentage that refers to the previous quarter or year. If we say GDP is up 3 percent, that means that the economy has grown by 3 percent over the last year.

The GDP growth for the US in 2011 is estimated to be less than 2 percent. Compare that with China, which had a GDP growth of 8 percent. A fast-growing economy like Brazil is expected to have an increase in GDP of 5 percent in 2012. Of course the United States is still a big economy; at 15 trillion, it's very rich compared with all other nations. Even at half that, at 7.5 trillion it's still huge. But with its tiny GDP growth, the United States faces a deficit of 1.5 trillion dollars.

Anticipating a future with little growth in sight, Thiel's betting on the unexpected is not unreasonable. The future is made up of both trends and the unexpected, so Thiel is looking for the unexpected: low probability, high impact sources for revenue opportunities. We've seen them emerge before.

Years ago in the IBM era, work with computers was almost exclusively a domain of huge, squeaky-clean office buildings dedicated to programmers and white-shirt, tie-and-collar folks. The notion that one could sit at a little 12-by-15-inch screen and access zillions of pieces of information would have seemed absolutely ridiculous. Yet here we are—not just making a living doing it, but giving rise to Mark Zuckerberg, possibly the world's youngest billionaire, who hasn't worked for IBM a day in his life.

In the 1990s the Internet industry was a lifesaver for the US economy. Firms like Yahoo, Netscape, and eBay emerged to match rising deficits with tremendous growth in web-related business. In the beginning years of the new millennium, however, we have only two growth firms: Google and Facebook. Wolf tells us this drop-off is a sign that the Internet industry has become a maturing market with little hope of answering the call for renewal of revenue growth that we expect from the economy. And there is nothing on the horizon.

How is this recession different?

The 2008 crash—creating more debt to solve debt

In responding to the financial crash of 2008, both the Bush administration and the Obama administration reacted decisively with a stimulus package; bailouts; and printing, borrowing, and spending trillions of dollars. But if the problems that led to the financial meltdown of 2008 were rooted in too much debt, does it make sense that the solution is more debt, especially when we have a deficit of 1.5 trillion?

.The experts tell us that one of the reasons for the financial mess we are in is the excessive spending and borrowing that was done over the last few generations. Well, if that's true, should we be pursuing more spending and more borrowing as an answer?

Economist Hunter Lewis notes that President's first budget, entitled "A New Era of Responsibility" proclaimed that it moves us "from an era of borrow and spend to one where we save and invest." Yet, incredibly, the budget then calls for an addition to the national debt of approximately $1 trillion a year. Why would Bush and Obama do such inconsistent things ?

Keynes went wrong-and took the rest of us with him

In adopting spending policies, Bush, Obama, and countless leaders of economies all over the world relied on prescriptions developed by the most important economist since Marx—John Maynard Keynes. Economist Hunter Lewis questions this wisdom in his book *Where Keynes Went Wrong*. One of the surprising things Lewis discloses is that Keynes had very little evidence for his theory.

Lewis debates the validity of Keynes's economics, starting with a review of the past century and proceeding up to the current crisis. Lewis notes that for years governments followed the Keynesian formula of providing the low-interest-rate environment that served as the very cause of the current credit crisis and recession. Still some progressive economists claim that the recent stimulus package didn't go far enough. Nobel Prize economist Paul Klugman proposes an increase stimulus input of 8–10 trillion dollars to save the weak economy.

Who's right?

Evidence and argument

There is some evidence that increased government spending in a recession is necessary to maintain the economy. There are cases where abrupt curtailment of government expenditures worsened the economy in a recession.

Progressive economists maintain that "an economy depends on the confidence of the players. If confidence has been shaken by too much bad debt, restore confidence by adding more." There is some merit in this statement. If you're out of a job and have overspent the little you had, the friendly presence of someone at hand willing to bail you out until you can become employed will certainly make you feel less desperate and give you more confidence in looking for a job.

Higher Taxes Ahead for US Citizens:

Increasing debt means accumulating a lot of interest that has to be paid off. If the economy is too weak to provide increased revenue for interest payments, it needs to increase taxes. The US population will soon be faced with higher taxation in addition to the possibility of mandatory fees for health insurance, which can be expected to rise annually.

Can it continue? End of Fiat.

Critics of Keynesian economy argue that the option of borrowing or printing new money may become a thing of the past.

> **Fiat money**—*money rolled off the presses, not backed by any precious metal, such as gold. The name comes from a parody on the creation of the universe by divine will: Fiat—let it be so.*

Every time we print new money, we dilute the value of dollars held by our creditors. China, for example, has about $3 trillion in US securities. In the past they have bought treasury debt to prop up the price of the dollar in order to help support their exports to the US. But it is possible that China could threaten to dump US debt on the financial market. At the current time, it's not to their interests to do so, but conditions could change that would make them feel that kind of action is warranted. In our scenario we explore those conditions.

Employment outlook

The Congressional Office of the Budget (COB) forecasts high unemployment rates until 2016.

2011	2012	2013	2016
9.2 %	8.2%	7.4%	5.3%

The Obama administration has been criticized for providing jobs primarily in government and industries heavy in organized labor. Public works have been especially favored, as have been the auto manufacturers, where substantial payments have been made to the United Auto Workers Union (UAW.) There is an obvious political advantage in doing this for the union workers that heavily support Obama. But what about all the other industries that could use similar help?

The Business sector response

Conservatives have argued that one of the biggest reasons behind a slowdown in the economy at this point in time is the inability of business owners to predict taxes lurking in the future. If they can't predict taxes, then they can't calculate profitability. The Health Care Reform Act, with its unknown costs, contributed greatly to this reluctance to hire workers. Of course it is possible that if businesses decided to ignore the uncertainty in taxes and proceed to hire workers, production would increase sufficiently to offset tax liabilities. But it's a risk businesses are unwilling to take, given the spend-free attitude of the Obama administration.

Free market

In addition to the economists that favored the Keynesian approach, there is another group that tends to be more conservative known as the Chicago School of Economics. One of its leading proponents is Nobel Prize winner Milton Friedman. The Chicago thesis states that "free and open financial markets would most effectively support market efficiency and stability, directing funds to the most profitable and productive uses."

Note that this principle stands in contrast to Keynes's proposition that government needs to regulate fairness in the markets. Many investors felt the financial markets could do with a little regulation. Banks did take a beating from unregulated trading— an area called the shadow economy.

> **Shadow economy**—*includes things like hedge funds, money market funds and structured investment vehicles.*

All these shadow economy trading funds were well beyond the reach of existing state-sanctioned monitoring and regulation as they grew to an excess of $10 trillion by late 2007. But government regulation, when it's possible, brings its own problems. Lewis asks, if the government needs to regulate fairness of the markets, what about the government itself being fair? How often are government officials influenced by politics? Do they truly make things fairer?

Regardless, the Obama administration has erected regulatory oversight of the shadow banking system, which was followed by a slew of other regulatory oversight agencies, giving rise to banking and financial community complaints of overregulation.

Decoupling of economies

One of the most important developments in the current financial situation is the decoupling of economies on a global level. This will play a crucial role in developing our scenario for the next 2000 days. By decoupling, we mean one part of the world has a booming economy while the other is barely moving. If we look at the world economies we find, for example, a fiscal crisis in the works for the European Union. Poor performers like Greece threaten to drag down countries with stable economies. In the case of Britain, we find that 50 percent of their exports go to their trading partners in the European Union. This is a barely growing economy. The much faster growing economies of China, India, and Brazil get only 5 percent of Britain's exports. It appears that Britain prefers the strategy of maintaining prices for fatter profit margins over going after the faster-moving new economies, where they could sell a lot more at a lower price.

What we're finding is that there is an uncoupling of the market response of Europe and North America economies as opposed to China and other emerging markets.

What's going to happen?
Our scenario based on the above financial considerations

Incoming taxes and costs associated with health-care insurance will be the leading financial stressors on the American population. Health-care plans will require participation of the general public and will involve mandatory payment of premiums. The administration touts two major factors that will bring health-care costs under control. The first is that savings will be realized through a more efficient delivery of health services. The second is that, through increased enforcement, fraud will be eliminated. If this is actually accomplished, it will be without precedent in health-care systems.

Our scenario adopts the CBO employment projections. We project the end of Fiat and the development of new debt constraints on the United States. Decoupling of economies on a global level will be the thing to watch.

With the failure of both Keynesian and the Chicago School of Economics as guides to the economy, we predict that new economic paradigms will develop. In our scenario we will offer consideration of a growth sector that will lead to a possible boom in revenue but not until 2019. It will develop as a united consumer response to coercive changes following a second Obama victory.

CHAPTER 4

Geopolitics

Questions:

Does the United States have to worry about China replacing them as the world superpower over the next ten years? Is the influence of the United States on the rest of the world really declining? What impact will the events going on in the rest of the world have to do with the US election and the changes that will occur in the next progressive rule?

Real-world effects

Years ago the above question might have been purely speculative, but today's headlines remind us of how interrelated we all are. As already noted, we have a $3 trillion debt to China, which in turn supports the dollar in order to boost exports to us. Have you ever had a problem finding "made in China" products in Walmart?

Sitting safely at home in your living room looking at CNN, the riots in Greece look like something far off, but (despite what politicians and economists tell us) the United States will eventually be called on to back the IMF bailouts of failed European Union economies like Greece.

All this means that if we're putting together a scenario of how progressive rule will affect our daily lives we can't just go on our merry way and forget about players on a global level.

Geopolitics

The business of looking at how other people's collective policy impacts your affairs is loosely defined as geopolitics.

> **Geopolitics**—-*traditionally defined as the study of the influence of such factors as geography, economics, and demography on the politics and especially the foreign policy of a state.*

In recent years the concept of geopolitics has received a revamped progressive interpretation.

NeoGeo: a new way of looking at things: Will France always be France?

What is this new geopoliticals and how does it differ from the above definition? Let's start with geography. The geography taught to most of us in the recent past concerned itself with the physical and cultural features of clearly defined countries. The new geopolitics (NeoGeo) challenges the very notion of a country. We always assumed that Spain will always be Spain and France will always be France. Not so, according to the NeoGeo. What we once identified as individual nations should be regarded as "space"; we must now question the concept of permanency. National identities are merely idealized fiction. Simply put, forget about the idea of a Jeanne D'Arc or the notion that France actualizes its independence through cooperation with divine will.

Also to be revised is our understanding of the cold war and other historical events. Gulags aside, the cold war was merely a fiction devised to feed egos. Nobel laureate Scholzynitzen may have personally found Soviet existence brutal and dehumanizing, but that's only him; it's only his opinion. Understanding NeoGeo will help you understand why Obama had no reservations in refusing to retain the bust of Churchill on loan from England. He has a progressive take on history.

Real-world effect of NeoGeo

To see how this kind of NeoGeo thinking plays out, just take a look at Europe. As result of a longstanding desire of for a united Europe, leaders from a number of countries created the European Union. The benefits included a common marketplace for member goods and services and a common currency, the Euro.

Recently individual member countries of the European Union developed financial difficulties that led to borrowing and increased obligations. There has been concern about this new development. If a country takes money from the EU, does that mean the European Union now calls the shots and dictates policy in that country? This could mean a real conflict.

Consider the case of Ireland. The Irish as a people are opposed to abortion and, in an agreement with the European Union, Ireland made honoring that tradition a condition for joining the European Union in treaties. Will increased obligations to the European Union affect that provision in the future? Progressive concepts of social change dominate the EU, and this would include applying the NeoGeo perspective of impermanence of countries. Finland has already expressed concerns over preservation of autonomy and self-identity as a nation.

Russia

It's difficult to map out how a future Russia will affect the United States. There is a segmentation in vision among the Russian leaders.

Some have a modern outlook and desire to see Russia cooperate with Western goals, but there is also a lot of resistance to that path. It is not at all clear how and in what ways Russia will join the West. In the matter of the Iran boycott, Russia joined the West initially but refused to approve subsequent sanctions. There is also the problem of Russian armament sales to terrorist-prone nations.

The political stability of Russia is also a question. Hillary Clinton joined others in protesting Putin's reelection bid that involved irregularities at the poles. This kind of criticism increases political tension in the former Communist state.

Multipolarity

Multipolarity one of the most explosive topics emerging in geopolitics. To understand why, let's take a brief look at the different divisions of world influence we've seen in recent history:

Bi-polarity: United States and Soviet Union created two separate and opposite spheres of influence on much of the rest of the world.

Monopolarity: With the fall of the Soviet Union, the United States remained the single biggest influence.

Multipolarity: Other regions of the world emerge to challenge the economic and military power of the United States and its global influence.

There have been several factors that argue for the loss of US influence worldwide. The report, "Global Trends 2025: A Transformed World," was drafted by the National Intelligence Council and forecasts events up to roughly 2020. The report sees a waning of US influence, particularly in Latin American countries, where nations have been meeting in groups without the usual US initiation and participation.

The hot economies in the Third World, such as Brazil, are another factor challenging debt-ridden, recession-strapped

US influence. Even so, Brazil's growth requirements need substantial investment to sustain GDP. But there is a strong possibility that another area of the world is heating up even faster economy-wise.

Get a hold of a world map and draw your finger in the shape of a big U starting at the northernmost point of China's coast and working your way down to the lower part of the Pacific that includes Australia and over to the western edge of South America and back up the western coast of North America. This curve and all the countries inside it is called the Pacific Basin, which is expected to become an area of extremely intense trading and investments in the next decades.

Taking advantage of this opportunity is likely to bring the United States in competition with China. While attending a summit in Hawaii, President Obama indicated that he was in Asia. His critics were quick to point out a defect in his knowledge of geography; however, his thinking of Hawaii as part of Asia is actually a modern perspective and will become an increasing reality with Pacific Basin economic developments. (I was told by friends that the Honolulu Police Department actually has investigatory powers in parts of Micronesia since they are, in fact, the closest resource. So thinking of Hawaii as Asia is not far off.)

China

China has become an important player in the US and European financial markets. The Central Bank of China holds substantial debt from both the United States and the European Union. Nevertheless, in contrast to several projections, our scenario does not see China becoming the dominant power replacing the United States in global influence.

First the United States represents the most efficient model of human consumption of products ever devised on this planet. Free men are able to make free choices in the marketplace and are free to engage in business without government interference. China needs our consumer frenzy.

It is said that China is a country whose sociopolitical development hasn't kept pace with its industrial development. This is certainly true in a country that places stringent control over the lives of millions of workers. This further implies that China is incapable of creating the overarching milieu that sustains the merchandizing and self-identity necessary in markets catering to a rapidly evolving culture. China can make significant inroads into construction and public works projects in places such as South America and Africa, but as these develop, it becomes apparent that China's influence lacks the capacity to creatively nourish human needs on a global scale. The fluidity of American merchandizing will make it a highly desirable target for products from China for decades to come.

You have to love the irony: China, a Communist regime will be the most serious opposition to the Obama administration's threat to end American freedoms. Our scenario tells how.

Islam

Readers of the 2000 days scenario aremay be surprised that I give little consideration to the Islamic world. Do I expect them to have no effect? The answer is yeah, maybe.

Westerners react with horror to things Moslem; this is not without reason. The event of 9/11, subsequent terror attacks, images of stoning innocent women (as depicted in *The Stoning of Soraya M.*), the deplorable honor killings of defenseless women as in Kingston, Ontario, the mosques where young men sit for hours listening to expressions of hatred for the United States, the persecution of Christians… All of this cannot be denied. Yet I must say that the appearance of an Obama-Biden bumper sticker fills me with more terror than any Islamic image ever could. Why? Two reasons.

First, Moslems are pro-life. The Muslim people, together with the Mormons, are the fastest growing populations worldwide and consequently Islam and Mormonism are the two fastest growing religions because they believe in creating life. As Peter Kreeft notes, the Moslems have been trying for centuries to take over Europe and

THE NEXT 2000 DAYS

have been unsuccessful. They are now replacing Europe with Islamic people not with the sword but with the new weapon: mothers.

In the Koran we find phrases showing great reverence for mothers, even the mother of Christ who seems to have a special place that supersedes even the mother of Mohamed. Who was it that spoke out at the international women's conference in Beijing against the proposal that all women should work to make abortion safe? It was a mother, the Moslem leader of Pakistan, who reminded women of the world that the ultimate victims of abortion are most often women. Abortion can never be safe. Consider how Turkey's entrance into the European Union would give Ireland another nation to speak up against the ratification of treaties that would include abortion for all members. I therefore consider the Moslem people as an ally to Christian civilization.

The second reason I find Islam far less threatening than progressives is because they have never really encountered a Christian nation. If that seems like a completely untrue statement, consider this dialog:

Party A	Party B
"I hate you."	"I hate you and your brothers and sisters."
"I hate you, your brothers and sisters,	"I hate you, your brothers and sisters,"
and your mother and father"	your mother and father, and your whole village.
I hate you, your brothers and sisters,	I hate you, your brothers and sisters,
your mother and father, your whole	your mother and father, your whole village,
village, and your country.	your country, and your children.
I love you.	I…

You see it doesn't work. Something happens. Of course you could go on hating, but somehow that seems all of a sudden to be an extraordinarily weak response. Love is always greater than hate. But in encountering Western civilization in modern times, Islamic culture has always found an consistent response of hate to hate. After 9/11, Islamic society found abundant examples of responding hate. A price was put on Osama bin Laden's head. But what would have been a genuine Christian response? Reading out of the Gospels we see things like love your enemies, do good to those who despise you, turn the other cheek. We've heard them all dozens of times.

What would have been the response of Moslems worldwide if the headlines after 9/11 read, The United States Forgives Osama bin Laden," "United States Wishes to Do Good to Osama bin Laden," "The American people Love Osama bin Laden." Would it have had any effect on the youth that opted to strap on exploding devices so they could retaliate against those who hated them? Who knows for sure? G. K. Chesterton has an often quoted comment: "The Christian ideal has not been tried and found wanting; it has been found difficult and left untried." Untried, so who knows for sure?

CHAPTER 5

Parties

Introduction to the US political environment

When Americans go to the polls in 2012 to vote for the next president of the United States, most will expect to find only two main candidates; this is essentially how it's always been. Two political parties, the Democratic Party and the Republican Party have dominated American politics since the American Civil War. The last time other parties played a role in the American presidential election was in 1852.

We are, however, living in a time of unprecedented changes in politics. With the integration of social media and increased media coverage, all aspects of the personal and public lives of presidential candidates are revealed with an intensity never seen before. Another big change: many longtime political observers were surprised by the participation of younger voters in recent elections. Those twenty-nine and under were, in fact, the only age block that showed increased participation since 2004.

The 2010 election

In November 2010, American voters put the Republican Party back in control of the House of Representatives by a surprising margin of 240-193, the largest Republican majority since 1947. Democrats still maintain control of the United State Senate, but their margins went from 60-40 to 53-47. So the 112th Congress consisted of a Republican House and a dramatically reduced Democratic Senate. This created new challenges for the administration.

This unprecedented response from the American electorate resulted from enhanced communication and interactive capabilities brought on by social media. The Tea Party movement, with its support from a mixture of Republicans and independents materialized out of concern for fiscal control. The movement emerged, to the surprise of many, as a spontaneous reaction of voters.

Since the 2010 election did not involve presidential candidates, there undoubtedly was less interest on the part of many who voted in 2008 and who will surely vote in 2012. (This might explain the drop in the youth vote by 60 percent from 2008.)

Media and social networking

Media and social networking are expected to play an important role in the 2012 election just as they did and in 2008. Among Internet users, 83 percent are between the ages of eighteen and twenty-nine. These overwhelmingly use social networking sites. The percentage drops to 51 percent for those fifty to sixty-four.

Note to parents: Expect to see your children on YouTube selling Obama's reelection if you don't approve of him.

The Obama campaigners will make an intensive effort to reignite youth for 2012 participation. Obama's Campaign Organizing for

America (COA) will deploy a social media strategy that combines innovative outreach techniques together with a focus on youth turnout. The key will be to ensure interactive responses from youth. Input from YouTube and foursquare will help identify, energize, and monitor potential voters, making them accountable for that all-important voting day in November.

The opposition

Of course the other factor in determining reelection is the strength of the opposition. One way to do this is to compare Obama with a generic, unnamed Republican candidate.

The president is well-known and defined; the candidate is not. Voters therefore do not have as strong an impression of what's on the other side. An October Gallup poll in October 2011 gave an unnamed Republican 46 percent of the votes; Obama was eight points back at 38 percent. If elections were held on the day of the rating, it might be predictive. But once the powerful progressive electoral machine is in place, it's an entirely different outcome.

As the presidential election of 2012 approaches, it appears that polling is less reliable. In the past, rating the incumbent began a year out from the election and, as each month went by, public ratings of candidates gave an increasingly better indication of the actual results. Presidents with approval numbers above 48 percent in a Gallup poll would win elections. Those with approval ratings below 48 percent usually lost. Conventional wisdom says that if voters don't approve of the job you're doing after four years in office, they usually don't vote for you. President Obama averaged a 41 percent approval rating among registered voters in his eleventh quarter in office; among independents it was only 38 percent. Is this a good indication of his reelection prospects?

I would say no. The reason is that it is very difficult now for us to extrapolate future election behavior from polling. We see a great fluctuation week after week as public awareness becomes exquisitely tuned to the most recent events getting heavy media coverage. Consider the following recent polls:

- In the Greenberg poll among likely voters, the race was tied at 45 percent each.

- The NBC/WSJ survey put Obama ahead of Romney by 2 points, 46 percent to 44 percent.

- A Pew Research poll in late September/early October came up with 48 percent for each man.

- A late-September Fox News poll had Obama up by 3 points, 45 percent to 42 percent.

- A similarly timed CNN survey showed Obama up by 1 point, 49 percent to 48 percent.

In addition polling numbers may not accurately reflect actual voter responses. One may not like or even have a particular dislike for a candidate at the time of polling, but deep down feel that one should vote for the candidate anyway. I would argue this is especially true in the case of Obama.

Third-party candidates will emerge and fall

In fact, within a certain range, the lower the ratings are for Obama, the better his chances for reelection. Why do I say that? It is because the lower ratings might induce a third candidate to enter the fray, creating the illusion that a third-party ticket would stand a chance. This would virtually ensure a victory for the progressive candidate.

Consider the divisiveness going on among the candidates. It's only going to grow worse as the nomination conventions approach. If Obama's rating goes into the low thirties, a candidate might decide to run as a third option, thinking there's a chance. This is what I call the *cherchez la femme* theory. The name implies there is a woman behind everything a man does. I have been told that running for the presidency is a kind of decision that takes place in the bedroom. It seems to make some sense, given that most presidential candidates are married men. One can imagine a dialogue like the following going on:

To husband: "Alice says Rick is going to run. Why should he run and not you? You're better than him. Remember Maryland? They said you gave the best presentation. You should run. Don't you want me to be First Lady?"

So the husband suddenly starts to imagine that he can be president of the United States and makes plans the next day to start running for office. But of course he can't be president and will find that out after he makes a nuisance of himself and wastes funds that could be better spent elsewhere.

The Electoral College

Some American voters are surprised to learn that when they go to the polls to elect a president, they don't actually elect a president; they elect an elector, who will in turn elect the president. There are 538 electors; 270 the of them are needed to elect a president.

Compared with electing someone to the legislature, which involves a direct election, the Electoral College method is an example of indirect election and is set up by constitutional provisions. Each candidate has electors assigned to him. If a candidate wins, his electors win and will cast ballots for him. If he doesn't win, his electors will not cast the votes; rather the electors assigned to his opponents will get to vote. Actually the way it's set up, electors are free to vote for anyone they wish, but the practice has been to vote for the specific candidate to which they have pledged themselves.

Is the Electoral College a good system? It certainly has its critics. Some claim it is archaic and inherently undemocratic, that it distorts the presidential race by giving a disproportionate influence to key swing states. It's proponents argue that the college protects the rights of smaller states, an important, distinguishing feature of federalism in the United States.

Of course, a candidate can win the popular vote and still lose the Electoral College. This happened to Samuel Tilden in 1876, Grover Cleveland in 1888, and Al Gore in 2000. But the popular votes and the Electoral College numbers usually come down on the same side.

There have been attempts to remove the Electoral College with a constitutional amendment, replacing it with the direct popular vote. No proposal has ever been ratified in Congress. Yet.

Futuring notes on political parties

The following is a recent prediction of 2012 elector breakdown by political observers.

270 votes needed to win

Obama	205	196
Republican Candidate	191	181

Under progressive rule we predict that the current electoral process is in jeopardy. If those in power believe the US Constitution is not absolute doctrine, then they will be ready to mold it as they see fit. We will shortly see what this means for the rest of us.

CHAPTER 6

Obama's Achievements

Obama is the first black man to win the office of the US presidency. Surely that is a remarkable feat. But in terms of futuring, it may turn out that history will record him differently. He is really just as much white as he is black, and it is only the current society's racist judgment that labels him black. Two hundred years from now, mixed marriages may be so common that it will appear that his nonwhite component is inconsequential. In addition Obama has yet to establish himself historically as president. By that I mean that if he doesn't serve a second term, he will indeed become known as the forty-fourth president, but if he goes on to a second term, the true character of his administration may become known. It may be revealed for what it is: the first triumvirate—the first three-man rule in American history.

Obama always has a very becoming demeanor, almost priestly in his appearance, wearing dark suits to give the impression of being more mature than his young good looks would indicate. Some describe him as being professorial. And then there is the frequently asked question: Was Obama really a law professor?

When the matter was initially investigated, the administration at the University of Chicago provided a written statement to the effect that he was an adjunct as opposed to a professor. A short time later a letter was put out by the president of the University of Chicago stating that he was indeed a professor. That should have ended the matter. Obama did in fact teach core law school courses. However, a behind-the-scenes interview with some members on the University of Chicago's board of directors revealed that special action was taken on Obama's behalf to gain the president's letter. One describes him as lacking any interest in teaching duties, even going so far as to claim that he was lazy.

Many of his fellow adjunct instructors would not regard themselves as professors, but the board stated that they willingly offered him tenure.

Obama achieves special recognition as the first person of African American ancestry to be president of the *Harvard Law Review*. However, it is difficult to find any articles written by Obama in the journal. The *Harvard Law Review* presidency is achieved by vote rather than the provision of extensive scholarly research publications in law.

The suggestion is that Obama, lacking extensive contributions and scholarly activity, doesn't really fit the perception of a law professor entertained by most of us.

The progressive defeat of Alice Palmer

Obama's entrance into politics was likewise amazing given his lack of experience in any kind of public office.

Alice Palmer was a well-known civil rights Illinois State Senator. She left the state senate to run for US Congress and lost. She then attempted to regain her position but ran up against someone who also had his sights set on the position: Obama and company.

Obama had the backing of the Alinsky progressive organizations, but little experience in any kind of public office. How does one go about winning if you're afraid you won't get public support?

The Obama group resorted to an often used progressive tactic: if you feel you'll have trouble defeating your opponents in an election, look for ways to disqualify them.

Andy Stern's Service Employees International Union (SEIU) supporters used the same tactic in the 2008 elections for the Local 61 delegates to the SEIU convention. Reformer Alex Hernandez led an opposition group that scored a surprising upset. They contested forty-nine slots and won thirty-three, a clear majority edging out Andy Stern's supporters. To bar Hernandez from serving as a delegate, SEIU suspended him from membership on charges of encouraging a decertification movement. Hernandez insists they were contrived, but by filing suit against him in state court, his opponents forced him to resign from his elected position as member of the local's board of directors. So much for the democratic reform movement in the SEIU.

In the same manner, Team Obama went to work on Alice Palmer, examining petitions in the courthouse filings, and, to no one's surprise, they found fraudulent signatures. A search of other signatures eliminated candidates from the ballot.

How did his organization know there would be fraudulent signatures on petitions? Well…Chicago politics? The progressives sacrificed one of the most respected legacies in Democratic politics in a primary for Obama.

Speech at Democratic Convention for the nomination of Al Gore

Obama gained national recognition almost in the same fashion as Robert Redford's character in *The Candidate*. Obama excelled in doing what he always does—performing according to a script. His speech at the convention gained him a national audience.

Obama and the powerful who back him

Early on in his life, Obama attracted the backing of the powerful. His application to Harvard Law was supported by recommendations of one of the most prestigious families in New York. A call from a member of the board of directors of the University of Chicago overturned an administrator's written statement. His announcement of candidacy for presidency almost immediately earned him a check from George Soros, one of the wealthiest men in the world. It was made out to him personally for the maximum legal amount.

Once he had achieved the office, Obama began to show a very unusual presidency model. Andy Stern and union leaders had the greatest access to the White House, while Obama barely seemed to meet with his own cabinet. Having pledged openness, Obama conducted his administration in such a way that it actually became more closed to scrutiny than that of his predecessors. Consider the length of time required for announcements after important events, something suggestive of extensive prepping, and the way they came out well-rehearsed like some well trodden statement out of a college dorm kabitz, almost always delivered with heavy reliance on teleprompters. Obama relied on teleprompters so extensively that he reread his own introduction when it appeared on the screen by accident. All this suggests a man that doesn't really think for himself.

It would seem then that the best-fitting model for the Obama presidency is a triumvirate, for the office of the president of the United States is held not by a single man but by a three. Who are they?

Obama is the Napoleonic front, the man of destiny, providing the panache, the bravado. But who are the other two?

Andy Stern, SEIU head, the muscle, represents the collective interests of unions and organizational programs with voter influence. He was recorded as the most frequent visitor to the White House when they kept logs in the early part of Obama's term.

George Soros is the third man, providing the cunning and economic resources.

It is not that these last two men are personally present in the White House but rather that they represent a constant influence in decisions.

Who is George Soros?

George Soros is one of the most politically powerful individuals on Earth. His personal fortune totals $13 billion, and he controls another $25 billion in investor assets through his firm, Soros Fund Management

In an October posting in *The New American* blog, Sam Blumenfeld reveals that "an equally significant source of Soros's power, however, is his passionate messianic zeal. Soros views himself as a missionary with something of a divine mandate to transform the world and its institutions into something better as he sees it."

The *Discover the Works* blog has compiled extensive information and analysis on Soros. It reports, "Since the mid-1980s in particular, he has used his immense influence to help reconfigure the political landscapes of several countries around the world — in some cases playing a key role in toppling regimes that had held the reins of government for years, even decades. Vis à vis the United States, a strong case can be made for the claim that Soros today affects American politics and culture more profoundly that any other living person."

Sam Blumenfeld also asks an interesting question: "…why did Soros decide to make Obama president instead of Hillary? The answer is simple. Obama was an empty suit, easily controllable by the master puppeteer. Hillary was too much of an insider Washington politician to be anyone's puppet. And women are much more difficult to control. And so, invisible Soros chose the best potential puppet at hand."

I would not agree that Obama is merely a puppet. I believe it is easy to detect his personal flavor of Alinsky training in the blend that currently directs the White House. But I think it's hard to deny the other forces at work.

News organizations are quick to point out that there is no direct connection between Obama and the various activities associated with George Soros. The Obama administration certainly enjoys certain benefits from allowing programs that they approve of to roll out under the auspices of George Soros. In the future we see no such luxury for Obama, and the activities of George Soros will be laid squarely at the feet of his administration. Blumenfeld suggests that one reason Soros's intimate connection to Obama is not yet readily available is due to another attribute Soros feels he has in common with the God of the Bible: a desire "to be benevolent but also invisible."

Achievements as president

Obama's achievements as president are listed on a website indicating the various "promises kept." He has been criticized by both conservatives and liberals—conservatives for the obvious reasons, and some liberals maintaining that he should not have caved in. Others maintain that, given the circumstances, he achieved a lot; to expect too much more is naïve. Some of the major results of his administration follow:

Regulation

> President Barack Obama and key advisers introduced a series of regulatory proposals in June 2009 addressing consumer protection, executive pay, bank financial cushions (or capital requirements), and expanded regulation of the shadow banking system and derivatives. The Dodd–Frank Wall Street Reform and Consumer Protection Act was signed into law in July 2010 to address some of the causes of the crisis.

Health care reform

> A comprehensive bill was passed.

Stimulus package

On February 13, 2008, President George W. Bush signed into law a $168 billion economic stimulus package, mainly taking the form of income tax rebate checks mailed directly to taxpayers.

On February 17, 2009, President Barack Obama signed the American Recovery and Reinvestment Act of 2009, a $787 billion stimulus package with a broad spectrum of spending and tax cuts. Over $75 billion of this was specifically allocated to programs that help struggling homeowners. This program is referred to as the Homeowner Affordability and Stability Plan·

Don't ask, don't tell repealed

This was seen as a victory for ending discrimination of homosexuals in the military.

Defense of Marriage Act

Obama instructed the US Department of Justice not to uphold this act, declaring it unconstitutional.

National security

Obama authorized the attack leading to the death of Osama bin Laden.

Futuring the Obama presidency

Both liberals and conservatives are puzzled by Obama. Conservatives see a radical racist socialist interested in taking the country way too far left. To liberals he represents "a disconnect between the transformation-promising candidate and the actions of the president who appears to be tolerant of, if not complicit in the system" he came to change.

After Obama's first year in office, Jon Meacham had this to say in early 2010: "Obama has failed a key test of Democratic leadership: the task of communicating and convincing a significant number of his countrymen of the wisdom of what he wants to accomplish. Given the president's oratorical gifts this is an odd developments, but there we are."

Actually I believe Obama has been remarkably consistent, perhaps more than any president in last hundred years. While his term of office thus far may not seem as great as supporters expected, they are a preparation for the most dramatic changes the nation has ever witnessed; Obama will be responsible for the greatest changes to the structure of the American Republic. However, before we address that, first we must explain how and why he will win the election of 2012.

PART THREE

Electing a President

CHAPTER 7

The Election of 2012

Obama's polls and ratings

Almost nightly for at least the last two years, Bill O'Reilly has taken on a stern look and repeated the same thing about Obama: He's in trouble. If he doesn't do something, he's finished as president. The folks are not going to elect him if this keeps up. On the *Sean Hannity Talk Show* the same kind of thing has occurred. Karl Rove would hold up a board with numbers: "No president with this kind of rating, this close to an election has ever been reelected."

Scenario Statement

Obama is not now, never has been, and never will be in the slightest danger of losing the reelection.

The public polls that seem to spontaneously self-generate at every turn are insignificant. The reason polls don't matter is because the Obama campaign does not move at a sustained, reasonable pace that has characterized candidate efforts in times past; it's a frenzy. The powerful machine will be set in place when it matters, right at election time. We have already explained that the lower the ratings, the better Obama's chances. Third-party candidates may emerge only to soon fall

The reasons Obama will win

First, the most important factor is an underlying confusion of morals symptomatic of many segments of American society. This is number one.

Second, the Hegelian imperative—the perception that a vote for Obama means moving with the tide of history—is powerful.

Third, the illegal population will increasingly access the American voting system.

Fourth, the lack of any creditable popular opposition presents little challenge.

Less important factors include voting fraud and intimidation resulting from the actions of unions and other left-oriented organizations.

Republican debates

The most powerful means of rendering the GOP meaningless is through the candidates' own words. The debates do not make better candidates. An official of the Republican National Committee actually claimed that it did. That is complete nonsense, as anyone can see by watching any of the sessions, during which candidates tear each other apart and then engage in follow-up press statements disparaging one another. The illusion is that once a front runner is nominated, the American people are going to magically forget all faults pointed out previously. Not!

Republican Party voters will choose their nominee for presidential election through a series of party primaries as well as national conventions. Not everyone is happy with the notion of primaries before the party national conventions. There are

Republican National Committee delegates who voted against the current primary calendar because they said it draws the primary season out too long. They argue Republicans should be fighting Obama, not one another, and this calendar isn't going to give them the opportunity to do that until much later. Also, some delegates claim this calendar makes it too tough on the candidates with little money or name recognition, favoring the wealthy and well-known.

The Republican contest began with a fairly wide field of candidates for presidency. Former Massachusetts Governor Mitt Romney, who ran for president in 2008, took an early lead in polls. He had the support of much of the Republican establishment. However, he swapped his lead new candidates entering the fray: Newt Gingrich, Rick Santorum, and Ron Paul. All candidates will campaign for months before a final party decision is made on which of them will face Obama in November 2012. Our scenario argues that it doesn't matter who is selected to be the Republican presidential candidate. It's even a mistake to waste time watching any of the debates. It simply doesn't matter. Obama never responds by argumentation in debates. He is always predictable, with his tightly canned replies. It is almost possible to have a contest to see who can predict the most phrases Obama will use.

National conventions

The Republican National Convention is set for August with the Democratic one a few weeks later in September 2012. Our scenario makes no prediction as to who will fill the Republican ticket or the Democratic vice president slot.

Date of election: November 6, 2012

The date of the election is set by law to be held on the first Tuesday following the first Monday in November in years divisible by four.

Who runs voting polls

Managing statewide voting operations is a complicated task. Both major parties take an interest in voting setups, which are the responsibility of the state local election commissions. Districts may use different ballot-casting systems. Voting day manpower requirements are huge; putting together a sizeable workforce for only one day is a mind-boggling human resource problem, and there may be a problem in finding enough qualified workers. Early voting places in Illinois are being run by noncitizens. Is that a problem?

A Republican observer brought this to the attention of the state voting commission. An investigation found that noncitizens acted as supervisors. One admitted to actually taking election materials home. In the November 2010 election, there were complaints of bias at these polls. Noncitizens are required to complete Federal I – 9 forms. Twenty percent of workers at three early voting election studies did not have the required declaration of eligibility. "Repeatedly, the human resources officials signed off on the. I – 9 form after the elections had occurred." Currently 18 percent of Illinois voters use early voting options. This number is expected to jump to 40 percent for the 2012 election.

Voter intimidation and fraud.

Progressives have taken preemptive measures by warning the public of GOP intimidation; translate that as attempts to review voting-place provisions. It is far more likely that voting intimidation will be carried out by progressives, as recent incidents involving SEIU suggests. As stated earlier, fraud and intimidation at polling stations will be a less important factor in election outcome.

Election forecast

As a result of the elections held on November 6, 2012, Barack Obama will be reelected president of the United States. Democrats will retain the Senate majority and will retake the House as a result of the "coattail effect" securing Democrat votes from those voting for Obama.

CHAPTER 8

The Illegal Vote

In his philosophy of history, Kant pointed out how the geography of the planet, as if by divine decree, predestines us to deal with the each other no matter how different we are as people. Because we live on a sphere rather than an infinitely large flat planet, we cannot disperse indefinitely, and thus contact with diverse people is ensured.

It has been suggested that to get some idea of the influx of immigration into the United States we should take a map showing the United States and Central and South America and turn the map upside down. You can almost sense the physical situation and imagine the hordes of people massing into the United States.

At the current time there is an estimated 10 million illegal immigrants living in the United States. About 7 million of them are involved in work of some kind. Many have lived in the States for decades, having children born and raised here, but they remain without legal status. Presidential candidate Rick Perry was criticized for his attempts to deal with the effects of illegal immigration in his state. Because he made education opportunities available to illegal immigrants, he ended up offering low in-state tuition rates for illegals, something that was not available to Americans from different states. The only other option, however, would be to maintain his state as a two-tiered society, one group having education and advantages and the other permanently uneducated and disadvantaged. The problem was not going to disappear, and Perry dealt with in a logical manner that was in the best interest of his state.

The real cause of overwhelming illegal immigration can be traced first to the exploitation of immigrant people by businesses looking for cheap labor and second to the efforts of the Democratic Party interested in creating a voting base. The progressive goal is to transform illegal immigrants into US citizens and sustain open borders to increase migration from impoverished countries south of the US border.

The encouragement of unrestricted movement from the south is integral to the progressive ideology, furthered by both the Obama supporters and George Soros, that countries are space without borders. In the Spring of 2006 many Americans were shocked by the extraordinary number of protesters appearing in public demonstrations against United States immigration policy, calling it unjust and punitive. Dozens of organizations **backed by George Soros** were involved in organizing the protests. What they wanted was amnesty, guest worker programs, a path to citizenship, and an open border.

Can Hart Schaffner Marx become more dangerous than Al Qaeda?

What is the effect of mass migration into a country? Places like Brazil recognize obvious threats from marginalization. To keep a large group of residents uninvested in the interests of the country they reside in is a mistake that can actually become a security risk to the autonomy of the nation. In a certain sense, the combination of marginalization and heavy use of illegal workers like the business Hart Schaffner Marx enjoys becomes more dangerous than Al Qaeda. Brazil found that establishing a mandatory stint in the army was an excellent way to socialize immigrants into the Brazilian culture.

Futuring

The question is *how is immigration going to affect US voting in 2012?*

In a June 2011 posting on the *Daily Caller,* Neil Munro suggested that the Obama administration was offering a form of amnesty for hundreds of thousands of illegal immigrants in an attempt to mobilize a wave of new Hispanic voters. The new rules were quietly announced in a "prosecutorial discretion" memo from top officials in the US Immigration and Customs Enforcement Agency (ICE) informing officials that they need not enforce immigration laws if the illegal immigrants were enrolled in educational centers or had relatives in the US military. Kris Kobach, Kansas Secretary of State, recognizes this as pushing immigration agents to be even more lax in enforcing the law.

It has been noted that the Hispanic vote could be crucial in determining results in swing states such as Virginia and North Carolina in the 2012 election. The primary documents provided new reasons for officials not to deport illegal immigrants. "The deliberate nonenforcement of immigration laws by the Obama ministration certainly seems politically motivated," Kobach believes.

But illegal entry into the United States also means illegal entry into communities. In the United States there are well-established networks to support illegal immigration. These can be found in almost every church and community center. In these cases there is always a discussion of rights for illegal immigrants, but there's never any discussion of responsibilities. In all the discussions that have occurred on immigration, nobody asked the immigrants for their input on how to solve the problems that each community is facing with the influx of immigrants.

This is little doubt that if they begin voting, immigrants would overwhelmingly vote Democrat. Why shouldn't they? If one political party consistently lets you know they want you and your family gone, deported, and prevented from opportunities in education while another political group wants to support you, which one would you vote for?

There is little doubt that immigration plays a role in elections. In the case of the iIllegal immigrants, particularly those who have been in the United States for long periods of time, there is a great likelihood that they will vote, despite their illegal status. In the States illegal immigrants have not deprived themselves of health care, public aid, nor education. There is therefore little reason to suspect that they should feel they should deprive themselves of participation in elections. In a sense, it is logical that individuals would and should have a say in what is going on in the community in which they live. Voting by illegals is therefore quite logical.

Former presidential candidate Al Gore maintained that in his bid for the presidency of the United States he was the real winner but the presidency was stolen from him. This is because he claimed to have the popular vote and should have been the president. But is it reasonable to believe that among those who voted for Gore there was a substantial number of illegal immigrants and therefore illegal votes?

It appears that illegal immigration has impacted election results in the past and can be expected to do so in the 2012 election. How large is this segment of illegal votes that are essentially unavailable to Democratic opponents? It has been estimated to be as high as 5 million, meaning that anyone opposing Obama in the election must be able to muster an excess of 5 million votes in order to offset the illegal votes. As it turns out, although the illegal immigration will affect the election, it will not be the major reason for Obama's reelection and should not affect swing states. What is also interesting in our scenario is that the impact of the incorporation of Hispanic populations into American citizenry will not unfold as progressives expect.

CHAPTER 9

The Hegelian
Imperative

All life and joy is motion.
That of time and vulgar souls is linear,
and so not without change of place;
and good to them is known only in the coming and going.
With souls of grace is not so.
They go about a center, which planetary motion is there joy.
They have also a self revolving motion, which is their peace.
Their regularity enables them to perceive the order of the universe.
Their ears with inmost delectation catch the
sound of the revolving spheres.
They live in fruition of the eternal novelty.
—Coventry Patmore

Medieval man, never thought the future would change all that much for his progeny. By the future, I mean that future here on Earth; medieval man was aware of another future, the one he kept close to his heart and mind, that hereafter, the desired bliss arising from traditional faith of an eternity with God: "The eye has not seen, nor the ear heard, nor has it entered into the heart of man…" There was, however, here on Earth, in man's daily life, the foretaste of this heavenly realm: the everyday pleasures of life, family, and yes, sexuality. All were a prelude to eternal bliss.

That all began to change with the Renaissance. Now the future could be better than the past, and—what was more—, men could change it, could bring it about. Man's existence now became the measure of all things. The ideals of eternity transferred into the present. The man that would be, became greater than the man that was. History was a pathway by which man created himself. Time was not a time for happy dwelling, but rather, time was the creative force of what was to come.

We have already made use of a watered-down version of Hegel's philosophy in identifying liberal and conservative political views. To the liberal mind-set, voting against Obama is like voting against penicillin. It is

- espousing ignorance

- voting for backroom "a la coat hanger" abortion for women

- bringing back Jim Crow laws

- the resurrection of slavery

For this reason, a significant number of Americans, no matter how critical they may have been of Obama's administration before the 2012 election, will again vote him into another term. This Hegelian imperative is the second most important reason why Obama will win in 2012. Not voting for him is like sliding backward. Obama's team seems to be keenly aware of this, which is why, in Obama's 2012 State of the Union address his speech began with the war cry: "We can't go back; we're not going back." As problematic as the first Obama term has been for some liberals, they regard it as a perch, a footing from which they can move forward out of the constraints of the Bush era.

A serious flaw in the thinking of progressives lies in their naïve understanding of history, which in turn reflects an even deeper problem, namely the serious deficits in contemporary institutions of higher learning. The once credible, established universities and schools of previous generations have fallen in the resources of scholarship and logic.

The fundamental flaw is assuming that they as teachers are the agents of education. Jacques Maritain notes that when we say man is a social animal, he is social because he needs teaching. The primary agent is not the teacher; it is nature, just as in medicine nature, not the physician, is the primary agent in healing. "In the same way," the catalog of Thomas Aquinas College reveals, "history itself will not make a well ordered mind. Rather, a cultured mind allows one to profit from the study of history." The faith that progressives put in history as a path to the creation of a new man is a result of the failure to understand both the nature of history and man. Nevertheless, it is sufficient to fuel a second Obama term.

CHAPTER 10

Confusion of Morals

In the 1950s high school students riding the New York subways would catch sight of an unusually dressed student. Unlike the others he wore a distinguished military uniform that rivaled that of a West Point cadet and produced envy in many a young man.

In those days the distinction of wearing that particular uniform belonged to a selected few, the students of Xavier High School. In the 1950s Xavier enjoyed an impeccable reputation for maintaining its Jesuit and academic traditions. It all appeared so attractive—**until you realized that the academy began from the proceeds of human slavery.** The uniform, the Jesuit tradition, the excellence in education-all seemed totally repugnant.

The facts of Maryland Jesuit slavery are now well documented in history, much of it contributed by the scholarship of the Jesuits themselves. But in the 1950s there was no real concern as to how Xavier came to be, nor any reason to feel the disgrace of its establishment through the proceeds from the sale of human life as property. That fact simply went unnoticed. The school, after all, enjoyed "an impeccable reputation for maintaining its Jesuit and academic traditions."

Brother Joseph Mobberly, S.J. (1818)

Question:	"Can a man serve God faithfully and possess slaves?"
Answer:	"Yes.
Question:	"Is it then lawful to keep men in servitude?
Answer:	"Yes."

The most profound example of mass neurosis

Then came the social awareness of the 1960s and the era of civil rights. It brought about what is probably the most profound example of mass neuroticism: the horror of any identification with racial prejudice. In many ways Xavier serves as a microcosm of that transformation.

In 1971 in the throes of the antiwar movement, Xavier demolished the mandatory rule of participation in JROTC. Suddenly, there was no all-pervasive reality of the Corps of Cadets. There was no longer that identification of manliness with the Jesuit tradition, reinforced by the Jesuits order's very name: "the company," armed and ready to serve the faith.

Along with that universal core requirement, the military academy perished, replaced by the image of a typical private school with ROTC on the side as an extracurricular kind of thing. One might well argue that even the Ignatian identity of the school had been affected by the declining number of Jesuits at the school and around the world. In attempts to offset this deficit, the lay faculty of Xavier claim to have consistently renewed themselves to the mission of Ignatian spirituality (as long as it was compatible with political correctness, no doubt.)

To New Yorkers long familiar with the institution's public presence, changes were noticeable. The image of the strict-appearing, ascetic Jesuit priest long associated with the school had been replaced with its more modern counterpart—the usually yellow-sweatered, often paunchy, private exclusive high school teacher laity. What is the school's mission today? Some observers find that when they review the published statements of the school they are unable to intelligently articulate the school's mission. Despite that, the school maintains that more students than ever understand the school's mission.

Peace and Justice

In many ways Xavier expresses the exquisite sensitivity to shame that almost subconsciously propels religious institutions today. The Catholic Church, as one of the most consistent religious institutions that articulates public statements, lends itself well as a prototype for study purposes. Note that the Peace and Justice declaration touted by the church coincides neatly with secular motives, pursued even at the expense of orthodoxy.

> Peace: Think of the antiwar, antinuclear movements along with Marxist attempts to defang the military of capitalism; in addition consider advancing the NeoGeo denationalizing of America and other countries worldwide.
>
> Justice: Think civil rights and the Soros-sponsored protests along with changes resulting from decisions by international courts of human rights.

Looking at the records, it's obvious that the Church has violated orthodoxy through these proclamations again and again. This is symptomatic of a confusion that has characterized American society for over half a century. Being wrong on the issue of slavery and having fostered racial prejudice in the past, the Church does not know what is right and how to keep from making similar social errors in the future. Like progressives they cling to the touchstone of social justice, but the real fear is not that of being wrong on a social issue. What is it then? Shame—it is fear of confronting shame.

What is one to make of the annual Jesuit-sponsored protest against what they perceive to be the former "School of the Americas?" When the civil rights movement came onto the

American scene, it motivated Jesuits to place themselves in the throes of organized crime-like conflict taking place in Central America, where they (apparently happily) caught deadly fire along with innocent civilians. They could have achieved the same martyrdom even more readily by standing up to drug lords in the neighborhoods of New York City, just steps away from a number of Jesuit educational establishments. In places like the Bedford Park parishes in the Bronx, for example, the drug cartels terrified parishioners to the point that they canceled religious parades and kept children from any public expressions against the evils of drug addiction out of fear of retaliation. But in those situations, those affected were Hispanic New Yorkers and the oppressors were not enemies of Marxist movements. The Jesuits seem to have felt a need to ingratiate themselves with the capitalist opposition. Sadly, there was not a single sign that any Jesuit supported victims in the decades-long, often violent struggle many families endured on the doorsteps of the Jesuit institutions in New York.

But how do Jesuits react to the ordeal in Central America? They erect crosses on every spot campus-wide, mobilize students, and annually assemble at a government site, declaring a protest against the taking of innocent life under sponsorship of the US government.

But what is this really all about? It's about shame. It's about the efforts Jesuits and so many others make to avoid confronting the shame that rightly falls upon them for the centuries of slavery they perpetuated in the Americas. In comparison with the School of the Americas, the deaths and human misery caused by Jesuit enslavement of countless lives in the United States and Central and South America is probably far greater than the toll attributed to the organizations they protest against. But like many, the Jesuits failed to realize that the Christian faith was not founded on an act of martyrdom; it was founded on an act of shame.

Take a look at any rosary, at all the religious jewelry promoted and worn by the masses and what do you see—dangling from the silver and gold chains is the figure of a naked man hung dying in one of the most disgraceful punishments devised by mankind. There was probably no greater symbol of shame in the Roman world than the cross. All that changed with Christ; the divine acceptance of shame is what created Christianity.

Immorality of America

This repression of shame produces a confusion that is easily exploited by progressive organizations. Besides the advantage of the confusion from shame avoidance, the progressive party has an additional advantage: America has become a place of intense moral decline.

If we had the correct orientation of moral values, we would not have elected someone like Obama into the highest office of the country. People often protest this statement, but I think many, like myself, are aware of their own moral failings, serious moral failings. One does not have to be innocent to see a crime, and, in fact, a criminal may do a better job of spotting it. But this widespread decay neutralizes our ability to resist progressive advances, particularly the Alinsky attack truth that feigns to support genuine human needs.

Alinsky will be discussed in later chapters, but Alinsky's technique is one of attacking an opponent with a truth even though one plans subsequent deceit and ruin. The institutional church is at a loss when it finds itself confronting Alinsky groups that associate themselves with all forms of compassionate, if not Christ-like, programs that have been missing in the church. But by understanding Alinsky, one recognizes the truth attack as only a preface; the underlying agenda is the destruction of man both physically and spiritually. If the church embraced shame, it would see that it has a tremendous contribution to make to current society; if the American church carried out this work, it would be far more beneficial than many of the destructive Alinsky projects they continue to fund. To put this in other words, we live in a world that endures a tremendous deficit as a result of the inadequacy of men of faith.

The abortion issue

In no issue is the confusion of morals more in evidence than the matter of abortion.

The first Alinsky attack truth is the observation that nature has given the task of nurturing human life in its earliest beginnings to women. At times, under some circumstances, the woman feels she and her child-to-be will suffer more if the child is born. It seems that stopping that life in the womb is an easy thing and a solution to all future problems. The Catholic faith sees this as a matter of orthodoxy, an intrinsically immoral act; it's the deliberate destruction of human life in its early stages.

Alinsky's second attack truth: women have been victimized by men in the past. Of course this is true. At times they have been demeaned, suffered lack of respect, lack of fairness in their wages, and intolerable employment situations where they have been victimized. Put all this together and you get where we are with the abortion issue today. The conclusion from the Alinsky view is that the abortion issue and the response arising from the religious faith of the church create just one more instance of injustice against women. The solution is to work against religious expression through widespread support for abortion, but they phrase it as a woman's right to choose. Notice that they never complete the sentence.

The most frightening thing about the entire abortion issue is not just that millions of lives are lost in the process, but rather the profound acceptance of the precept "pro-choice—a woman's right to choose." This is the acceptance of a profoundly illogical statement. It doesn't say *what* it is that a woman has a right to choose. Does she have a right to choose to burn down buildings, blow up bridges, murder husbands…what? Isn't it the right to choose to terminate a human life?

Kathleen Sebelius, current secretary of the Health and Human Services, has stated that science shows that the availability of abortion promotes women's health. I suppose one could apply the same reasoning to the need to promote suicide. Statistics show when people eliminate themselves, they solve problems of depression and mental illness. Should we then promote suicide as a statistically justified means of promoting health? Don't be surprised to learn that there is, in fact, a plan to do just that among progressives, starting with severely disabled veterans.

Nonetheless, it seems a very unnatural thing that it should fall to the state to have to intervene in the matter of policing a woman's abdomen. In fact abortion, as a matter of intense debate, shouldn't be the real issue. Abortion is really just a small part of the progressive agenda as set out in the Jaffe Memoranda, discussed in later chapters. Again it is the avoidance of shame once again that creates such an ineffective response from the church.

Consider Cafardiansm, a concept suggested by the statements of a *Catholic, staunchly anti-abortion,* Obama supporter. His reasoning is typical of many academics. It is a form of rationalization that degenerates easily into pragmatism. It begins with what is already in one's heart, a strong desire to be trendy and articulate the progressive Alinsky agenda. One wants to be right in the eyes of the politically correct world, though what is really at stake is the avoidance of shame. The human heart will not let shame in, so this is avoided by a self-mesmerizing episode of prayer and conscience examining, allegedly in the light of the Holy Spirit, but that same Spirit apparently leaves orthodox Christianity in darkness in this matter.

In Cafardianism one also manifests a deficit in an education that fails to allow one to place Obama's presumed pragmatic background in the setting of Alinsky's rules. Since these poorly educated academics don't realize that those following Alinsky don't have to be truthful, they are easily misled by Obama's statements. Cafardi refers to Obama's insistence that, through his efforts, he will decrease the number of abortions. But a simple review of the Planned Parenthood Jaffe Memo will show this is not the intent of the organization that Obama strongly supports. The intent is to decrease the human population. In supporting Obama, one supports those goals.

It is for the above reasons that I place confusion of morality as the most important factor in Obama reelection.

CHAPTER 11

Women Voters

Among voters no group is as predictable as women. In the 2008 election, 56 percent of women voted for Obama. We predict that in the 2012 election women will again overwhelmingly vote for Obama by the same amount or even greater.

Why do women vote for Obama?

Women share the same motivations as the general public in selecting candidates, but they tend to be more affected by the amorality factor than by the Hegelian imperative. Women tend to be less intellectual in politics than males. They tend to go for more concrete and practical motivations, which is why they are more susceptible to the progressive mind-set.

Consider the progressive trade-offs of modern women, what they sacrifice in exchange for gains in freedom and equality. They have bargained away the higher intangible realms, a deal that sits well with the Obama agenda. As part of reelection efforts, the Obama campaign will stress the administration's appointment of two new female justices to the Supreme Court. The passed health care legislation focuses on providing services to women, centered around their the control of their reproductive capabilities. And a recent seventy-seven-year-old's triumph in seeking a fair pay reimbursement law for years of inequality marks a victory for women's rights and equality in the workplace.

In addition, the Obama group is preparing to launch a powerful pitch machine that will involve woman-to-woman contact with a leadoff by Michelle Obama. Last, but of some importance, is the cosmetic affect of the Obama candidacy. Women are easily swayed by his attractive appearance and youth. As noted before, pre-election polls contrary to the above forecasts are a poor prediction of actual voting activity at the time of election.

Of course, in trading off traditional values, feminism has incurred some liabilities along the way. Among these has been the adoption of the male role. As feminism develops, its deficits in fulfillment will become more pronounced over time. In creating equality between moral worth and a paycheck, women have sacrificed traditional values for "bourgeois careerism." They sacrifice the higher dignity of devoting oneself to family, church, and a community of neighbors.

Futuring

Our scenario predicts that feminism will actually be a relatively short-lived movement coming to an end by 2020. The reason for its extinguishment is rather simple: successive generations will find careerism less rewarding than women do today.

Nature itself will also pave the way for the termination of feminism. It will become increasingly difficult for society to maintain that the myth that male and female roles are interchangeable. In almost all cultures recorded by history, that equality has been shown not to exist. Men, by their nature tend to be more aggressive, and one only has to look at the crime rates to reinforce that idea. Violent crimes are much more likely to be perpetrated by males than females. In addition, as Robert Kraynak points out, the progressive establishment of feminism is artificially sustained. It is highly dependent upon the ideology, namely, the progressive belief that the sex differentiation like identification of nationhood is a social construct only. As this ideology falls, so will the pillar of feminism. Today's technology masks sex differences, making things easier, and less heroic, than in the past.

The de- religioning process supported by the pragmatic philosophy is another important pillar in sustaining feminism. Along with the social and scientific advances, including the new atheism, there is a diminishment of patriarchal authority long associated with traditional religion. This will reverse as pragmatism wanes. With the onset of a severe social crisis, the pillars of feminism will collapse. The severe challenges will come by way of financial destruction and life under progressive totalitarianism, a regime hostile to family life. In society's attempt to resolve this crisis, women will appear more powerful, but not through bourgeois careerism—, but rather through their presence in the home and direction of community action.

PART FOUR

The Progressive Ascendency

CHAPTER 12

The Arc Begins

"I do solemnly swear that I will faithfully execute the Office of the President of the United States, and will to the best of my ability preserve, protect and defend the Constitution of the United States."

On January 20, 2013, on the steps of the Capitol Building, Barack Hussein Obama will take the above oath, officially initiating his second term of office. But who will administer it to him? The chief justice?[1] A federal or state judge? The Reverend Jeremiah Wright? Or perhaps a family member,[2] Michelle or Misha?[3]

None of these possibilities are without historical precedent. The Constitution of the United States requires the president to swear or affirm to a specific oath, but there are no mandates as to who must swear the president in, or where the oath need be administered. Given his penchant for flouting tradition, it may be expected that Obama is not likely to go for a traditional repeat. The Constitution, moreover, does not require a Bible or any book. It might even be done on foreign soil.[4]

Likely sentiments in January 2013

Let's examine what the atmosphere of early 2013 will be among Obama supporters and opponents.

Voters for Obama

By the time of the inauguration on January 20, 2013, much of the euphoria from election night has subsided. That victory was hailed a triumph over the Tea Party, Wall Street, and all other conservative groups incurring the disfavor of progressive supporters. True, a remnant of jubilation persists, of course, but the more knowing progressive supporters are, at some level, beginning to confront reality:

1. They have elected a president that thus far has appeared lacking in leadership ability.
2. There is considerable reason to lack confidence in his ability to effectively respond to problems.

But all that lies on a deeper level. On the surface is the renewed hope that this executive's past merely sculpts out the dimensions of the ruin caused by the previous Bush administration, and, given time, this president will prove himself.

Voters against Obama

What about the opposite pole? How do conservatives feel now that Obama has won again? We find a much muted anti-Obama populace. Having experienced the frustration of hoping so long and working so hard using the electoral process to end progressive rule, they realize it was to no avail. Many who evaded politics in the past have sacrificed wealth and time to support a political candidate for the first time in their lives. Now, completely burned out, they find that all their efforts amounted to nothing.

The opposition feels a loss of power. They have begun to seriously question whether they will ever again achieve representation through the election process they so firmly believed in.

The progressive arc

So now that the second term of Obama has started, what's next? It is ironic that while the opposition is thinking of loss and powerlessness, the triumphant progressive leadership is becoming more fearful than ever of losing power. The 2012 election was a pushover compared to the transformation phase that lies ahead.

For the election, all Obama's supporters had to do to overcome the Republicans was watch them trip over themselves in serial contests of one-upmanship. After months of debate, of tearing each other apart, the one who emerged in shreds was still tagged with all the things that are wrong with him. At that point, thanks to his self-serving colleagues, everyone knew why the Republican nominee was not the most suited for office. Of course, they tried to close ranks and, in ludicrous fashion, promote the damaged goods nominee. No thanks.

(It is certainly possible that opposition to Obama may not even close ranks. A third party candidate, as we previously mentioned, will further ensure an Obama win.)

So the election in 2012 was a given. Now the progressive party must vigorously pursue a more difficult agenda that will require substantial steps to achieve power. The progressive leadership realizes it will never again have such a great opportunity to achieve its goals, so leaders must take bold steps to pave the way for their vision. What are those steps?

Introducing backcasting

Perhaps we can best develop the progressive action that will unfold by using a futuring method called backcasting. In **forecasting**, one looks at things in the present and predicts what might happen: Will stock prices rise? Will the employment picture improve? In **backcasting**, one starts with a vision. (How does the person in question want things to end up?) Then one comes up with the steps needed to achieve that result, develops a sequence for the steps, and puts them in the format of a scenario.

We can apply backcasting to the progressive administration in January of 2013.

What are the progressive goals for the next 2000 days?

I have identified what I believe are the most important objectives of Obama Two:

1. Eliminate criticism of the administration's agenda through media control.
2. Develop social policing.
    *   Control the market response so as to avoid green company bankruptcy.

    *   Enforce restrictions on energy usage at the individual and organizational levels.

    *   Get the populace to inform on people who lack sufficient intelligence or have misinformation that prevents them from supporting government agenda.

    *   Ensure population control agendas identified in the Jaffe Planned Parenthood Memorandum. (See Appendix.)

3. Achieve diversification through the regulation of the personnel composition of all businesses, universities, and health-care entities.
4. Establish a social hierarchy with a privileged class for government and union officials.

5. Denigrate classical Western heritage by diminishing ideas of the absolute and supporting an international cooperative in denationing established states.
6. Terminate the democratic process as it allows unintelligent masses to block progressive reforms.
7. Perpetuate progressive control of government.

Of course, it is one thing to come up with a list; it is something else to be able to offer evidence that each and every one of these objectives are legitimate statements reflecting the vision of Obama Two.

Eliminate criticism of the administration's agenda through media control

Media control is an important part of the agenda. We need only to look at previous attempts by the White House to isolate Fox News. Obama's statements on local control of broadcasting by FCC hint at a more radical agenda yet to come.

Develop social policing

The Obama administration can barely contain its desire to enact **social policing**. The perception here is that people are lazy and poorly educated in matters of science and in the necessity to commit to green technology. There are abundant statements that support mandatory changes in population behavior. Obama's commitment to Planned Parenthood can hardly be doubted.

Achieve diversification through the regulation of the personnel

The Health Care Act contains provisions for mandatory diversity that reflect racial bias, even according to the Equal Rights

Commission. Penalties for failing to fulfill diversification mandates can be found in several programs supported by Obama.

Establish a social hierarchy with a privileged class for government and union officials

The president of SEIU, Andy Stern, was the most frequent visitor to the White House. Obama has made public statements of support for SEIU, granting them exemption from the provisions of the Health Care Act. He has advocated the revamping of government programs for youth and the cancellation of student loan obligations for government workers.

Denigrate classical Western heritage

In chapter four, we introduced the modernist outlook for geopolitics. Obama's adoption of the NeoGeo mentality was reflected in his decision not to retain the bust of Sir William Churchill and his appointments of transnational advisors Harold Koh and Eric Schwartz.

Terminate the democratic process

When Obama *opposed secret ballots* in union elections, alarms should have gone off for the general public. Advocation of antidemocratic measures demonstrates that Obama views the American representative processes are flawed and are in need of reform or outright elimination. Consider statements by North Carolina Democratic Governor, Beverly Perdue, suggesting that elections should be suspended—or the thesis offered by progressive thinker Peter Orszag in the September 2011 issues of the *New Republic*: "we need less democracy." It is reasonable to expect this sentiment to grow and, coupled with the support of Andy

Stern and others for a five year plan, it will threaten the future of the electoral process.

Having set forth the objectives, we now turn to the methods that will bring all this about.

Notes

(1) By established tradition, the chief justice administers the oath. On previous occasions, federal or state judges and even nonjudges have done the job. By convention, incoming presidents take the oath of office by raising their right hand and placing the left on a Bible. But other books have also been used: John Quincy Adams swore on a law book. A Roman Catholic missal was used on Air Force One to swear in Lyndon B. Johnson. Two Bibles were used in the oath taking of Dwight D. Eisenhower, Harry S. Truman, and Richard M. Nixon. And, true to his progressive leanings, Theodore Roosevelt used no Bible at all when taking the oath in 1901. Obama may well be eager to make the inauguration an occasion for demonstrating diversity through changes in the inauguration ceremony. If he elects to use a book this second time around, it is possible Obama may elect to use non-English and even non-Christian texts for the oath. (Wikipedia; Oath of the Office of the President of the United States. See also below.)

(2) In 1923, Calvin Coolidge was first sworn in by his father, a justice of the peace and a Vermont notary public.

(3) It would, of course, not be the first time a woman administered the oath, in as much as Sarah T. Hughes, US District Court judge, swore Lyndon B. Johnson into office aboard Air Force One following the assassination of John F. Kennedy.

(4) In 1853 William R King took the oath of vice president on Cuban soil.

CHAPTER 13

Methods Part I—The Alinsky Heritage

What follows is for those who want to change the world from what it is to what they believe it should be. —Saul Alinsky

Obama's method of creating change—Alinsky's Rules for Radicals

We set out a pretty radical agenda in the previous chapter. Making it all happen requires a powerful method. Obama believes he has just the thing: his old guidebook from community organization days, Alinsky's *Rules for Radicals*. Without some understanding of this work, nothing Obama does will make sense to you; study it a bit and everything he does makes sense.

Who is Saul Alinsky? Saul David Alinsky was a Jewish American writer, considered the founder of modern community organizing. His ideas were later adapted by some US college students and other young organizers in the late 1960s and formed part of their strategies for organizing on campus and beyond. Mention the name Alinsky and most college students will immediately associate it with his most notable work *Rules for Radicals*. The heart of Alinsky's rule is the concept of "a people's organization." Its purpose: "to wage war against all evils which cause suffering and unhappiness…to fight for those rights which insure a decent way of life."[1] Note the theme here: Your suffering and unhappiness are not of your own making. An evil force is to blame. A decent way of life is a right due to you for just being you. You just have to fight others to get it. This kind of mentality underlies much of the development of social thought underpinning progressive programming.

Introducing the "rules."

"*The Prince* was written by Machiavelli for the Haves on how to hold power. *Rules for Radicals* is written for the Have-Nots on how to take it away." Alinsky makes a nice comparison to Machiavelli in the beginning of his work. If it seems a little pretentious to compare his work with that of one of the most important works in political literature, just keep in mind that this little text of Alinsky guided the likes of Obama into the most powerful position in the world. In fact, *The Rules probably say more about us as a people than it does about Obama.* They are based on keen observation of our behavior in a free society.

What set Machiavelli apart from political thinkers during and before his time was his insistence on looking at the world when acting as a ruler. The Platonic ideal, the concept of a perfect world, guided men like Aristotle and Aquinas when they spoke of the virtues that a leader should possess. Machiavelli stuck the prism of the real world before would-be rulers and said this is what you should do because this is what rulers actually do (or haven't done) thus far. Virtue then becomes dictated not by ideals but by experience, and experience is not necessarily all that nice. Take, for example, the rather stark view on lying, which shows what happens if one lies rather than discusses why one shouldn't lie: "One who deceives will always find those who allow themselves to be deceived."[2]

This experiential notion clashes with the venerable concept of absolute values, an important heritage in Western civilization. To redeem the fall of absolute values, Machiavelli offers a remarkable justification, which has accompanied every expression of progressive rule since: *the salvation of the people.*

Put yourself in the position of someone living in Italy at the time of Machiavelli. First, there was no Italy, just divided, independent, ferociously competitive city-states. Shortages of food were everywhere. If you wanted to eat and feed your children, your city-state had to prosper by successfully competing with other city-states for an economy that would eliminate stark poverty and starvation. And who would do that for your state? The Prince.

Now, if your prince is going for the goal, how badly do you want him to win? Remember what happens to your family if he fails. If you're living in Florence, the heck with Verona and all the other vicious, thug-led city-states. You want your vicious, thug-led Florence to win. Machiavelli's *The Prince* is merely a statement that a man's gotta do what a man's gotta do. Put it another way: the plight of the HAVE-NOTS depends on the success of the HAVES. Does the end justify the means? Hell, yeah!

The concept of relative value carried over into Alinsky's rules. The collective dependence of the people grants freedom of conscience for acts carried out for a given cause. Alinsky claims he developed his rules after countless hours of studying manifestations of discontent among the young. He recounts how, at the end of the 1968 Democratic Convention, teary-eyed youths beseeched him for counsel. The party had failed to listen to their views and represent them in the final platform. What really drives youthful rebellion? According to Alinsky, it is the rejection of the following:

- materialism

- bourgeois middle class values (work hard for a living; start a career)

- respect for political leaders (think wars and race conflict)

- respect for parents (I suppose one could include procreation itself?)

Simply put, the fault lies with the "system," and the rejection of all of the above eventually extends to every part of the system.

What is Alinsky's solution to overcoming the system?

Alinsky's advice to the teary-eyed youths was that the next time the Democratic Convention rolled around, they should "Be delegates."

That seems like a tall order for young people attending college, looking for any kind of employment to survive, but Alinsky saw a way to make things happen. First he made a distinction between what he calls the real and the rhetorical reaction of youth. He points out three basic reactions of the youth to a chaotic world.[3]

1. Cop out—The youth is faced with a world he rejects, panics, and turns away from its challenges in hopelessness.
2. Take-on cop-out—The youth says, let me try some constructive response. The response quickly fails. The youth then cops out.
3. Berserk—The youth reacts with rage, violence, and unproductive, antisocial behavior.

The fourth alternative

To the above reactions, Alinsky offers the fourth alternative—the attack from within.

The attack has three characteristics. The first was communication. To be listened to and taken seriously, the would-be changer of society would need both the traditional *eloquentia perfecta*[4] that marked an educated man as well as the ability to convey a healthy dose of realism. Therefore second characteristic was the ability to see hurt in the lives of those needing change,the ability to rub red the sores of other people's misery. And lest they be morose and unattractive, Alinsky insists on a third characteristic: that humor be a constant feature of their presentation. Flag-burning and other signs of outright disrespect for the established government were prohibited. Alinsky reminded his disciples that they were going to use the excellent opportunities offered by American society to change it.[5]

Reformation begins with recruiting a popular base. One of the greatest obstacles to radical transformation is overcoming people's fear of change. Networking allows a changer to make inroads into existing structures, existing churches and community organizations, for instance.

The Satanic attack

Alinsky's tactic for motivating the community is a never-failing one—Satanic Truth. Now when I use that phrase, the word "Satanic" tends to be an intellectual turnoff. What is meant by Satanic Truth, however, is that one attacks with a truth even if one ultimately aims to deceive. Spiritual writers have often noted that demonic encounters usually begin with a statement that goes right to the core of the soul being tempted.[6] It is interesting to note that *Rules for Radicals* originally included a dedication to Satan, but don't go looking for it in the pages of the later editions; it was removed.

Consider Alinsky's preamble to the rules:

> In this book we are concerned with how to realize the democratic dream of equality, justice, peace, cooperation, equal and full opportunities for education; full and useful

employment, health, and the creation of those circumstances in which man can have the chance to live by the values that give meaning to life.

One can hardly disagree with those goals. How does one achieve it according to Alinsky? "Create mass organizations to seize power and give it to the people." For all the talk of eloquence, like all progressive agendas, Alinsky's plan is one based on coercive force, not reason.

The truths of dissent

Here are some examples of Alinsky's attack truths. The objective was to agitate, to create disenchantment and discontent with current values in order to move the audience to create meaning in life.

- The environment is being destroyed.

- Military conflict should stop. Innocent lives are being lost.

- People are forced to live in black, Latino, and Puerto Rican ghettos created by the system.

- Migrant workers are deprived and exploited.

- The suffering in Appalachia is appalling.

- There is racial hatred.

- There is prejudice against women.

- White people are too rich; black people are too poor.

- Too many black people are in prison.

- Ignorance, disease, lack of health care, starvation, and corruption plagues the Earth.

The target audience for the attack included youth, activists, and people that could be converted into activists, such as ministers, teachers, and parent groups. The goal was to get people to respond either affirmatively or at least retain a nonchallenging attitude.

How these methods were implemented will be discussed in the next section on Alinsky's protégé: Barry Obama.

Notes

1. Saul Alinsky. *Rules for Radicals*. This Chapter contains extensive reference to this text.
2. Machiavelli, Niccolo. *The Prince.*
3. Consider this a parody on the Gospel of Luke 8:5.
4. See "Your Jesuit Education" at http://www.measuraplena.blogspot.com/
5. Consider the piety of the fleeing from Troy. Virgil's *Aeneid.*
6. References to Satanic attack with truth can be found in a number of publications, including William Blatty's *The Exorcist*, C. S. Lewis's *The Screwtape Letters*, and Fr. Bartholomew J. O'Brien *The Cure of Ars.*

CHAPTER 14

Methods Part II—Obama: The Rules Applied

Obama adopts the Alinsky method

A brief look at Obama's organized application of Alinsky will be extraordinarily useful in forecasting the events of Obama Two.

Obama began his career as a community organizer with a Chicago organization known as the Developing Communities Project (DCP). The DCP was developed by the Calumet Community Religious Conference. It claimed to be a faith-based organization, yet it espoused the model of community agitation of Alinsky, a confirmed atheist who believed in nothing beyond the here and now.[1] In the DCP, organizers entered lower socio-economic neighborhoods and practiced the "stir things up" method. They knew how to "rub raw the sores of discontent," in Alinsky's words. The job of the agitator is to make everyone aware that they are, indeed, truly miserable. And all that misery is the fault of unresponsive governments and big greedy corporations.

The dialog between agitator and victim proceeds as follows:

Leader: "You are miserable."
Victim: "Yeah, I guess."
Leader: "No, you really are, and other people are the reason for your misery."
Victim: "Really?"
Leader: "Absolutely, and together as a group we can make demands."
Victim: "Cool.
Leader: "Demands will be met because of the self-interest of the Haves. They don't want to see all us black folks making a god-awful stink on their doorsteps or in the press. They'll grant whatever it takes to get the harassment to stop."
Victim: "Way cool!"

Ryan Lizza records in the *New Republic* what an early Obama mentor, Mike Kruglik, had to say about young Barry Obama:

> He was a natural, the undisputed master of agitation, who could engage a room full of recruiting targets in a rapid-fire Socratic dialogue, nudging them to admit that they were not living up to their own standards. As with the panhandler, he could be aggressive and confrontational. With probing, sometimes personal questions, he would pinpoint the source of pain in their lives, tearing down their egos just enough before dangling a carrot of hope that they could make things better.

So he knew how to ferret out pain in their lives… I wonder if Obama's own childhood prepared him for this kind of sensitivity, the knack of realizing how pain is kept deep inside individuals. The Harvard graduate called the Alinsky program the "best education I ever had."

Obama, the Alinsky chief executive

When Obama finally achieved the presidency of the United States, he began almost at once to implement Alinsky principles. The basic Obama format was as follows:

1. Begin with the Satanic Attack.
2. Bait the opponent into reacting. Focus on the attacking truth.
3. Most important: Do not to resolve the issue, and prevent your opponent from resolving it as well. This method takes away an opponent's ability to create an agenda.

It's easy to find examples of how Obama applied this method. Remember how, early in his administration, Obama and company harped on the idea of torture? What is the Satanic Truth here? Well, torturing another human being is hardly a civilized act. Torture had almost certainly been going on during the previous administrations to extract information about terrorist activity, and some members of previous administrations believed that certain aggressive tactics, such as waterboarding, should not be called torture but rather coercive interrogation.

Obama, as commander in chief of the armed services, could have resolved this issue through leadership. Simply make a clear statement to the effect that the United States no longer sanctions torture, and state explicitly what is to be included in the definition of torture, including waterboarding. But if he did that, he would put an end to the debate, drawn a line in the sand. From here on after, no more torture, defined as written. He could even have gone to his Democrat-controlled Senate and House to enact laws prohibiting torture.

Why didn't he?

Well, that would have meant a reprieve for those who had any association with torture before the law was passed, including members of the Bush administration. The directives and laws would, as is usually the case, begin at a certain point in time.

Members of the former administration would be immune to Obama's retaliation designed to impress world leaders.

Consider, instead, how this plays out. Obama generalizes that the United States doesn't torture, based on some unspecific existing law. He makes vague statements without addressing the specific issue. His opponents are trapped into defending torture of their fellowman before the world community. His attorney general can put the entire Bush administration on trial as war criminals.

The method works well. This is why it's important not to resolve an issue once it is raised. Obama has demonstrated this repeatedly in his administration:

- He helped pass health-care legislation, leaving payment as a hotly contested issue in dozens of state and district courts all over the nation.

- He agitated the poor and lower middle class with the notion that the rich don't pay their fair share, but blocked any real attempt on tax reform legislation.

- His administration sued states attempting to deal with uncontrolled illegal immigration but refused to enforce border security or negotiate immigration reform legislation.

- Early on in his career, he opposed any payment of reparations for slavery, stating that that would put the issue behind us and impair the ability to agitate based on history.

Obama's critics on both the right and left complain of his weak leadership. To the right, he appears to be leading the country away from its traditional values. To the left, "he seems a tragic failure, a man with so much potential who has not fulfilled the promise of change that partisans predicted for his presidency."[3] The truth is, however, that Obama has achieved exactly what he intended to do. He has divided the nation in a way it has never been divided since the Civil War. He has brought about power-ful tensions as a result of sharpening resentment between classes and races. In Obama's second term, this extraordinary upheaval will be exploited.

Who is Obama?

There has never been a president as predictable in both word and action as Barack Obama. Yet, for all that, he is a mystery that no biography can even hope to penetrate.

In his review of Obama's *Audacity of Hope*, Fr. William Barron makes some interesting observations about Obama's discussion of the Constitution.[4] As a pragmatist, Obama believes that the Constitution does not reflect absolute value and presents this in one chapter of his book. A few pages later, he comes across Harriet Tubman and other abolitionists, and seems to realize that they acted out of absolute values, suggesting that, sometimes, absolute values are acceptable. As Fr. Barron comments, "you can't have it both ways." He notes that Obama encounters this discrepancy in the topic of abortion, an issue that Obama seems to struggle with tangentially throughout the book. Does Obama perceive and yet resist the line of argument that goes from the opposition of slav-ery in the nineteenth century to the opposition of segregation in the '60s to the current day opposition to abortion?

If this is correct, this is a striking analysis since Obama is one of the most radical supporters of abortion, even opting for infanticide in the case of children that have survived an abortive procedure. He denied their right to life, something his fellow Democrats were reluctant to do.[5]

According to nurses at Christ Hospital in Chicago, survivors of abortive attempts were gathered up with biohazardous mate-rial, soiled linens, and urinals, and dumped into a dirty utility room, where the infants would struggle, squeak, and attempt to cry until their eventual demise, which could last as long as an eight-hour shift.[6]

Obama and infanticide—a pathological narcissist or victim of neglect?

Obama was the only state senator to speak out to promote this matter of denying newborn infants the right to life. Many put this together with their perception of Obama's coldness, and some observers have actually diagnosed him as manifesting pathological narcissism.[7]

Obama worried that legislation protecting live aborted babies might infringe on women's rights or abortionists' rights. It would lead to the unraveling of the logical structure underpinning abortion as women's health. His concern was unwarranted and overestimated the intelligence of the pro-choice populace in this issue.

But despite the temptation to label Obama as heartless and pitiless, I think that a little dabbling into psychoanalysis may give us another point to consider. Instead of just seeing Obama as merciless, consider that *he actually identifies with that struggling infant dying in filth.*

In 1995, Obama said, "My individual salvation is not going to come about without a collective salvation for the country..." and again in May of 2008, "Our individual salvation depends on collective salvation." To understand these rather curious statements, we turn again to the teachings of Alinsky: "The practical revolutionary will understand Goethe's 'conscience is the virtue of observers and not of agents of action.' In action, one does not always enjoy the luxury of a decision that is consistent with both one's individual conscience and the good of mankind. The choice must always be for the latter." Note the subservience of conscience to the perceived common good. Alinsky continues, "Action is for mass salvation and not the individual's personal salvation. He who sacrifices the mass good for his personal conscience has a peculiar conception of 'personal salvation': he doesn't care enough for people to be corrupted by them."

Barry Obama, the child who was left behind by his parents; Barry Obama, the struggling infant dying of neglect among filth and refuse. How else can he legitimize these actions except through the collective salvation of the masses? How else can he legitimize his denial of right to life to unwanted infants? How else can he accept and forgive what absent parents have done to him?

Behind strut of confidence as chief executive is the acceptance and forgiveness of those who neglected him and, for himself of those he would neglect and eliminate. His lean, almost priestlike demeanor clearly sets him apart from other presidents. His daily devotion to physical conditioning and personal habits deserve admiration. With the exception of smoking, he is a model for imitation, even by his opponents.

It is always possible that Obama could be converted, could renounce evil, could accept transcendental reality like a Paul or Augustine; he is young enough. What an asset he would then make for good! What an inspiration for youth it would be to see a young president lead from creative instinct rather than an exploitative mentality. Instead, we reluctantly forecast an entirely different future for Obama.

Notes

1. When asked, Alinsky would say, "I am a Jew."
2. http://www.discoverthenetworks.org/Articles/bobamasunlikelypoliticaledu.html
3. Kloppenberg.
4. http://www.youtube.com/watch?v=MvissOHjmxM
5. Jill Stanek from World Net Daily states, "BAIPA (Born Alive Infant Protection Act) sailed through the U.S. Senate by unanimous vote. Even Sens. Clinton, Kennedy and Kerry agreed a mother's right to "choose" stopped at her baby's delivery.

"The bill also passed overwhelmingly in the House. The ProChoice organization, NARAL went neutral on it. Abortion enthusiasts publicly agreed that fighting BAIPA would appear extreme. President Bush signed BAIPA into law in 2002." http://mydryfly.wordpress.com/2008/02/21/obama-and-live-birth-abortion/

6. http://www.youtube.com/watch?v=BYRpIf2F9NA

7. http://nocompromisemedia.com/pages/Understanding_Obama-The_Making_of_a_Fuehrer.html

CHAPTER 15

March–July 2013—The Fairness Doctrine

It might appear to some, that when a government takes action to limit the survival of a broadcast source simply because it doesn't like the way it criticizes it, such a government acts in violation of the concept of freedom of speech and freedom of the press. Yet if we backcast from the progressive goals, we see that this is precisely what is required to eliminate criticism of the progressive agenda. The progressive goal for the good of everyone is to stop misinformation that is oppressing the public; give voice to the oppressed; and overcome deficits in reasoning and science.

The Marxist media concept

The first thing we need to look at is a very simple idea known as the "Marxist media concept." Consider that we live in a free society. If an entrepreneur wants to, he can apply for and, if approved, operate a broadcasting enterprise. He decides on the content programming he wants. If the market likes it, he'll get an audience along with advertising revenue and be able to survive and maybe even make a profit. If the market says "not interested," the business won't succeed. That's just the way things work in a free society. Fox News appealed to a large enough audience; it flourished. Air America didn't; it went belly up.

While the successful broadcast producer may have the ideas and creativity to meet market demand, the progressive government has its own interests, which they claim to pursue on behalf of the masses. What is the next crucial step? *The government uses its political power to determine the content of private broadcasting.*

The plan is to gradually replace the survival-by-market criteria with political mandates. For a time, the government will permit operation according to the market, but, at some point, the content will be so controlled that the market support will substantially decline. Options for the government at that point are to either sustain the enterprise with taxes or shut it down.

That's the plan. Very simple. It's going to happen, and the entire scheme begins, to no one's surprise, with an attack with truth.

Broadcasting attack truth

Following Alinsky means attacking with a truth, then leading the unsuspecting into a position they might not ordinarily take. Consider Obama's statement to the Federal Commuications Commission in September 2007. Who could disagree with the statements put forth in his opening paragraph? The limited airways should be open to everyone, but local commercial radio and TV stations have ignored community groups and nonprofits. Broadcasters, because of their influence using publically regulated airways, should be held accountable for ensuring "the vigor and variety of public debate" on important issues?

To ensure representation of multiple perspectives, in 1949 the FCC enacted what has been known as the Fairness Doctrine.

In those days three major networks (NBC, ABC, and CBS) dominated news delivery. The possible misuse of the public license of these three organizations to present biased agenda concerned the FCC. For that reason, they created the regulation known as The Fairness Doctrine.

The regulation really said nothing all that controversial. It aimed to afford reasonable opposition for the discussion of conflicting views of public importance.

What's wrong with the Fairness Doctrine?

At first, the Supreme Court favored the ruling, upholding its constitutionality in a 1969 case, but by 1974 the court became concerned about the implications of the regulation in view of the First Amendment. It found the Fairness Doctrine failed to encourage discussion of controversial issues; it actually inhibited the "vigor and variety of public debate." Broadcasters wouldn't say anything about issues, lest they violate the regulation.

With the proliferation of media sources in the 1980s, the Supreme Court felt the scarcity of media underlying the doctrine was flawed. In response, the FCC began to reconsider the rule in the mid-80s, and ultimately revoked it in 1987 after Congress passed a resolution instructing the commission to study the issue.

Today, the technological advancements are staggering in comparison to what was available in the late '40s, and the prospect of government bureaucrats policing the airwaves to decide what is and what is not correct comes off as downright creepy.

Obama and the Fairness Doctrine

In 2008, the Obama administration realized that criticism of the opposition would not go away with the absence of Bush; it intensified. With Democrats in power in both houses, Pelosi as speaker of the House, and Harry Reed in the Senate, both moved to restore the Fairness Doctrine without success. Obama himself opposed the bill.

Why was President Obama against the Fairness Doctrine?

To begin with Obama did not wish to appear outrightly to be against free speech. The administration already caught enough heat from the Tea Party Movement. Then, too, broadcasters like Fox, (which would be a prime target for the administration's implementation of the Fairness Doctrine) were proving very useful. They gave increasing amounts of exposure to emerging candidate opponents. The diversity would assist in diluting the opposition in a future presidential election.

Probably, the best reason Obama opposed the doctrine was that he had a better way of dealing with critical broadcasters, and the Fairness Doctrine would only impede its effectiveness. That new way was federal localism.

Federal localism

What is federal localism? Essentially localism is another FCC regulation, but it works on a one-way basis. Only local communities and progressive nonprofits can claim bias. The rule is rather vague but essentially states that if broadcasters want to get or keep a license, they must serve the interests of local communities. Former FCC Commissioner Robert McDowell warned that localism could also be used to wedge in principles of the Fairness Doctrine: "The government would be compiling data as to what kind of content you were airing and whether the government thought that was appropriate content," McDowell said. "It could be political speech, it could be shows on baking or gardening. But we don't know where the government is headed."

Who decides whether the local interests are served? That would be defined by a three-member vote of a five-member committee. If you guessed that three members are Democrats, you would be right.

Localism *IS* a better deal for the Obama administration

To head his transition team after the 2008 election, Obama appointed John Podesta, president of the Center for American Progress, to the task. Right off, he noticed there were too many conservatives on the radio.

Now the average person would say that had something to do with the market for conservative talk, but to Podesta this was in his estimation, because there was not enough localism required by the FCC.

Again, notice here the use of the Marxist media concept. Podesta didn't say, let's give money and air time to local entities and let them compete for an audience. Rather he asked, how can we get on the backs of those who are able to make the industry work and dictate what we like on the airways?

Charles Benton heads the Benton Foundation. Like most progressives entities, it proclaims the Alinsky attack truth. He claims that there is racial and gender discrimination in the media, which his organization seeks to eradicate and then "create our culture." Now, even if you buy into the attack truth, you might not want to end up spending your days in Benton's culture; nevertheless that culture must be something Obama finds highly attractive. Podesta tapped Benton's director and general counsel to head the FCC transition team.

Broadcasters become cautious of localism

Thus far, the FCC has made only recommendations, such as the creation of advisory panels comprised of broadcast professionals and community groups. In anticipation of further action by the FCC, however, airway entities have begun enacting token tribute to the threat of localism.

Comcast, in preparing for FCC approval of a merger with NBC, agreed to partner with NBC local entities. The terms of the deal made it obvious that Comcast had no real interest in local community broadcasting; they included a slew of provisions in the deal that would allow it to get out of the partnership. FCC dockets are filled with nonprofits' "Nice Things" letters that appear to have been dictated by broadcasters to ameliorate any future complaints of insufficient localism.

Standing by and observing all this are the progressive scribes. Their criticisms appear to be seething with a desire for government coercion. When you read what they have to say, you get the feeling they salivate just thinking of the day when the government comes knocking down broadcasters' token efforts, penalizing them for "deep hostility to the slightest amount of public interest legislation."

Media reformer Josh Stearns, considered by many to be a far-left commentator, agrees that Comcast's sudden commitment to local nonprofits seems suspicious, given that the media giant blocked local activity in Philadelphia. Comcast "included elements of localism to placate policymakers concern." Commentator Matthew Laser ridiculed TV-station endorsements by Blind Babies Foundation of Oakland and Goodwill Industries of Mid-Michigan.

Futuring the broadcasting sector—a new aggressive agency

Far more aggressive measures will be launched by both FCC and a rather new innovation in agency control devised by the administration under the guise of consumer protection. The two will start to act at the beginning of 2013 and will become full-blown by 2015.

By July of 2013, a loss of commercial markets due to increased progressive programming will seriously impact advertising revenue. Progressive financial measures, including fines and loss of revenue, will impact radio stations. Also affected will be smaller radio stations unable to meet the financial provisions of the Performance Rights Act, which requires payment to recording artists when the stations play the artists' song. While this makes sense for larger stations, smaller ones will be pressured to shut down due to lack of funds.

However, the final blow to free broadcasting in America will result from a new transition. However legitimate the movement to promote local community expression may have been, it still left intact the ability of private ownership. The new movement will question why "the 99 percent" shouldn't have ownership of national media assets. We can look at the progressive treatment of Fox in the next chapter as an example of how this will occur.

CHAPTER 16

December 2015–January 2016—The Fox Demise

The most vocal critic of the Obama administration is by far and away Fox Broadcasting. Almost nightly, Fox stars Hannity and O'Reilly successfully assemble viewers across the globe to hear comments that frequently reflect unfavorably on the White House. While he was running a live TV broadcast, Glenn Beck shocked his audience by exposing every possible relationship he could find between Obama and the progressive left. So for Obama's administration, Fox offers an unprecedented double whammy: the combination of heavy criticism by a show with highly successful ratings.

Who is Fox?

Fox News, frequently identified as Fox News Channel (FNC), is the dominant cable news network in the United States. The cable and satellite television operation is owned by News Corporation, with Australian-American media mogul Rupert Murdoch retaining controlling interest in the conglomerate that covers forty countries worldwide. Fox News has received considerable criticisms for its conservative political positions. The critics claim that public interest is at stake with nightly distortion of the news on Fox programs. In replying to such charges, Fox states that news reporting and political commentary operate independently of each other, eliminating any bias in the news reporting.

Of course, there are other news organizations that could also be charged with bias. MSNBC, for example, reflects unquestionable bias in programming. Just a few minutes of the *Ed Show* will tell you of that. O'Donnell, another talker, rarely presents both sides of an issue. The reason given by producers is that the opposite side has no merit and is not worthy of consideration. The *Rachel Maddow Show* does, to some degree, air views opposing the progressive formula, but it falls far short of presenting a balanced perspective. One could say there is a war going on between conservative and progressive broadcasting. If it's a war for numbers, then Fox is clearly the winner. Yet there are clear signs that Fox is an endangered species. Below are the incidents that herald what is to come in the future of Fox.

Early steps toward the fall of Fox

When Obama and company came to Washington in 2009, they began what was a longstanding progressive dream—to curtail freedom of the press. It's certainly true that other White House administrations had their problems with news organizations, but the case of the Obama progressives was different. Obama threatened the very existence of critical public expression, and the insidious strategy to bring Fox down will go a long way toward accomplishing that.

In Obama's first term, the administration advanced an interesting theory: freedom of the press only applies to so-called "qualified" news organizations. First, they would attempt to neutralize the effects of Fox, declaring Fox News was not a voice on parity with other news organizations. Second, they would use blogs to erode public confidence in the enterprise.

Fox News is a species other than that to which freedom of the press shall apply.

White House official Anita Dunn took the lead-off. As communications director she referred to Fox News as "not a news network." She asserted, without offering any evidence, that "Fox News often operates as either the research arm or the communications arm of the Republican Party."

On ABC's *This Week*, on October 18, 2009, David Axelrod White House Senior Adviser had this to say about the station where millions of people get their news every night: "They're not really a news station." He told George Stephanopoulus, then with ABC, "You ought not to treat them as a news organization."

What about those live reports coming in from correspondents risking their lives in dangerous parts of the world where war and other catastrophes were all about them? Axelrod chillingly says, "It's not really news." (John Stewart maintains they do it just to keep the Fox viewers as the "most misinformed" international audience. Wow.)

Now, if the likes of Axelrod had made such unintelligent comments in generations past, the public would have had immediate concerns about allowing that administration to continue serving the American people. But it went virtually unnoticed. On one of those rare occasions in which Obama himself was called into account for White House infringement of the press, Obama replied with his usual lack of logical thinking: "We call it like we see it." Apparently, the press is not allowed to call it like they see it.

Advancing the theory of *freedom of selected species of the press*, Rachel Maddow chirped a *Sesame Street* parody while validating the administration's eroding of the freedom of speech: "One of these things is not like the other." One of these does not need to be defended under the First Amendment. Anyone who gets information from one of these needs to have their thought processes examined. Note to Rachel Maddow: Nobody fought to defend someone's definition of a news organization.

Any rag that calls itself a newspaper, any mottled poster pasted up in a public forum, is protected by freedom of speech, and almost every self-respecting reporter (Maddow apparently the exception) would stand up for their right to free expression. To the surprise of the administration, this fact was demonstrated shortly after Axelrod's comments to ABC's *This Week*. It was the matter of Ken Feinberg.

Pay-czar scandal

Within days of Axelrod's statements, it was reported that Fox had been specifically excluded from joining a pool of reporters conducting interviews with administration official Ken Feinberg.

Kenneth Feinberg served as the special master for the Troubled Asset Relief Program (TARP) Executive Compensation (the treasury department's "Executive Pay Czar").

According to the *New York Times*, "Fox's television news competitors refused to go along with a Treasury Department effort on Thursday [October 22, 2009] to exclude Fox from a round of interviews with the executive-pay czar…" Fox News Channel's James Rosen reported that this backlash forced the Obama administration to reconsider its position on the matter: "The Washington bureau chiefs of the five TV news network consulted and decided that none of them would interview Feinberg unless Fox was included, and the administration relented…"

Faced with this reversal, the administration tried to back-pedal and claimed there was never any attempt to exclude Fox, but White House memos obtained under the freedom of information act confirmed that Fox was singled out. This confrontation was, no doubt, a setback for Obama, but in a few months the White House received a coup in its effort to dispose of Fox. The Fox enterprise began to self-destruct on its own.

Fox phone-hacking scandal

Beginning in July 2009, Rupert Murdoch faced allegations that his companies had been regularly hacking the phones of public citizens, celebrities, and even royalty. This led to the closing of its British tabloid, the168-year-old *News of the World.* Murdoch faced police and government investigations into bribery and corruption in the United Kingdom. In the United States, the FBI launched investigations, as did Attorney General Eric Holder, who vowed to investigate the Murdoch Empire from the top "down to the janitors." With this kind of scandal calling into question the integrity and future of News Corp, investors reacted: company shares fell by more than 13 percent within days of the allegations.

With the news of the Fox scandal, the progressive blogworks went into action, targeting Fox advertisers, calling on them to cease using Fox. They launched a campaign encouraging investor withdrawal. The California Public Employees' Retirement System (Calpers) and the California State Teachers' Retirement System (CalSTRS) are two huge California pension funds with investment in Fox. Both organizations stated they would vote against the reelection of Rupert Murdoch to the board of his media conglomerate, News Corp, at upcoming board meetings.

The most serious threat to Fox survival, however, will be political, not financial.

The attack on Fox shifts: *Color of Change*

The *News of the World* scandal provoked protest demonstrations from a number of leftist groups. Rashad Robinson relates that part of the strategy was to expand the protests into neighborhoods where a number of wealthy New Yorkers lived. According to the *Color of Change* blog, the group "had plenty to protest" at the Murdoch home.

Protestors complained of "race baiting" on Fox News, and said the Fox News agenda was dividing America. By "dividing the country," the *Color of Change* apparently meant that Fox News was not supporting the culture change advanced by the Benton Foundation. Of course, many viewers turned to Fox in the first place because they were opposed to the social notions of Benton.

The group also protested on the grounds that Fox would "do anything for profit."

Wealth distribution fairness

This concept that profit is evil is an excellent tool for agitation in the hands of progressives. The Occupy Wall Street movement in 2011 blamed the economic problems on the pursuit of profit by private industry. Note that, as this movement begins to intensify in 2012, there will be a shift away from the previous progressive discussions regarding the rights of expression and the necessity to affect programming. The agenda now turns to the right of actual possession of broadcasting assets by private parties. Why should 1 percent have the right of ownership of assets while 99 percent go wanting? This 1 percent concept was a powerful attack on private ownership.

Scenario: how Fox falls

So how does the mighty Fox empire end up disappearing from the American political scene? First, we look at the mounting financial pressures that will surely impact the Murdoch enterprise well into the first year of Obama Two administration. We can continue to expect political outrage and investigations over the phone-hacking scandal. When a corporation is embroiled in the kind of scandal that Fox has, you can expect that any deals in the works will come under scrutiny. As a result of the scandal, Murdoch was forced to withdraw an "ambitious bid to take over Britain's top broadcaster, British Sky Broadcasting." Murdoch will continue to be at a disadvantage in remaining competitive.

Increased localism will play a more important role starting in 2013. The perceived FCC constraints on the Comcast/CBS merger will start to look like a mild example of localism pressure on dealmaking. We can expect pressures to intensify, making deals of any kind impossible. Investors will begin questioning the future of Fox in this new climate.

Investors are already asking what the broader impact of the scandal will be on Murdoch's global News Corp empire, which includes the Fox network, cable channels such as FX and Fox News, television stations, the 20th Century Fox movie studio, and newspapers around the world, including the *New York Post*, the *Wall Street Journal*, and the *Sun* in the United Kingdom. Murdoch's access to capital markets can affect projects across the board.

The end of moderate localism

As the much-ridiculed tokenism comes to a close by the end of 2015, aggressive localism will turn full bore on Fox. The coupling of Obama's "tax the rich" campaign with Soros's Occupy Wall Street movement will create sufficient pressure on community advisory boards to make radical concessions. The first stage will stress the need to address lack of community expression and to end divisive programming. The second phase will involve increasing agency regulation, including the erection of new regulatory subunits that will police the airways for any evidence of alleged divisive, racially-biased or gender-biased broadcasting.

A new fairness doctrine emerges

The new programming will result in decreased viewership. A drop-off in advertising will follow, and investors will start to bail, thus increasing Fox's financial problems.

The 2014–2015 demonstrations will become increasingly focused on the need for mass ownership of public utilities under the cry that It's not fair that only a select few should control the people's airways.". Obama will pick up the theme and include it in several of his public appearances.

After exhaustion of local measures to eliminate as many conservative talk shows as it possibly can, the progressive party will encourage the FCC to draft an updated version of the Fairness Doctrine. This rule will formally dictate the composition of the board of directors for broadcasters like Fox. A Congress greatly influenced by the concept of mass ownership of broadcasting will pass the FCC legislation. Investors will continue to flee.

Change of board of directors

Fox's response will include concessions to avoid threats of regulation and to improve investor concerns. By January 2014, changes in programming will lead to an increasing amount of time devoted strictly to news coverage. Fox will make a move to put politically neutral members on the board, and Chief Executive Roger Ailes will resign in late 2013 or by the end of January 2014.

Criminal militia

Since the welfare of the masses is at stake, the progressive administration will resort to coercion to achieve its objectives. This will bring into being the components of the new civilian militia. The Occupy Wall Street nonprofit organizations of 2011 and 2012 will develop into the government's enforcement arm for media control. Violation of broadcasting standards, such as depriving community nonprofits and minority groups of broadcast time will incur criminal penalties. Hearings and trials will result. The big names of the Fox era will be happy to run from the media in exchange for whatever liberty they may enjoy in Obama's second term.

The folks, as we'll see, will shortly be looking out for themselves.

Chittumism

As unbridled progressivism erodes the fundamental liberties of everyday life, the loss of freedom of the press will logically yield the loss of what I call the "freedom of the read." The responsibility for cultural violations by organizations like Fox will be passed along to individuals that subscribe to the organization. This concept of putting the blame on those who read is designated *Chittumism*, based on the teaching of Ryan Chittum, who stated that Murdoch's media turns "celebrities into nonpeople undeserving of basic dignity and decency, and anyone who buys rags like the *News of the World* (or, say, *US* or *Star*, or who watches TMZ) is complicit in this." The principle is simple: if you read what the progressive administration finds offensive, you are just as guilty as the party that prints it.

Fox's demise

By November 2014, Fox will be a much changed entity. By January 2015, the former cable news source for millions will be virtually unrecognizable. *By the end of 2015, there will be no major organization in the United States that's critical of the progressive agenda.*

CHAPTER 17

The apolarity of broadcasting

Some may wonder what it will be like in the Fox-less era. No O'Reilly or Hannity or any of the recognizable stars of Fox nightly. Political junkies will suffer. But the falloff of programming will be gradual rather than a sharp decline. Celebrities like O'Reilly are typically absent on segments that occur close to holidays, and viewers will become acclimated to substitutes who are less critical of the administration and progressive actions. To see what will replace programs on Fox, merely look at channels like MNBC and ABC and imagine a more ethnically diverse hosting with an increasing percentage of women heading presentations.

Personalities like Anne Coulter and Michelle Malkin will restrict their exposure. Look for the most talked about celebrities to be much less political. Overt statements against the individual government administrators will become rare due to enhanced opportunity for civil and criminal lawsuits.

Elimination of Maddow-like programs due to lack of targets

Rachel Maddow made a career of ridiculing selected targets of the Republican Party and other entities hostile to the progressive agenda. By 2014, such targets should be a rare feature of political life. True, there will always be a bumbling van der Lubbe to prey upon, but the shift of power will render nonprogressive personalities insignificant and boring, though not without some danger. It will be remembered that Maddow did grant some exposure to opposite points of view The administration in Obama Two would prefer that no mention of any kind be given to the opposition. For that reason, Maddow's program will be targeted for removal shortly after the decline of Fox.

Whistling prevails

A woman recently told a reporter how attending a meeting at the University of Chicago brought back horrific nightmares of her youth in Nazi Germany. She had earlier attended a meeting at which a somewhat conservative speaker was among those to appear. As the moderator began the introduction, the screech of whistles began from some in the audience. The whistles began and never stopped. The woman had seen this before: it was a progressive street tactic of the National Socialist Party to keep the opposition from being heard. And seeing it used again, hearing the painful shrill against a speaker at the University of Chicago, brought it all back to her. She remembered precisely what it was like.

This is still one of the most effective techniques employed by liberals to control debate, and no one does it better than actor and writer Lawrence O'Donnell, progressive whistler par excellence. I once observed him going six minutes straight in an interview, every single exhale roped to an incessant recicitive. No matter what the interviewer asked him, O'Donnell never exhaled without the same monotonous beat. It was impressive, albeit chilling, to see such extraordinary resistance of O'Donnell to the intellectual reception of ideas of another human being.

O'Donnell will be retained. His job will be to ejaculate a series of attack truths each evening. He will whistle well.

The naturalness of truth

What's wrong with stating the truth? There is a certain naturalness about truth in the human existence. Incessant attacks are unnatural, however. For example, while it is true everyone defecates, to focus on nothing but statements about a person's defecation, while they may be true, are none the less an unnatural distortion of the reality of existence.

"God is mad as shit."

The progressive applications of truth find easy roads into other areas, such as religion. Consider Rev. Jeremiah Wright as an example of how truth can be consumed by religion. To accomplish this, the first thing you need to do is to shift from the basics of Christianity to the construction of an anthropomorphic God; that is, a manmade God. This is what is called the "God is mad as shit" theology.

Wright is pissed off at white America; therefore, God is pissed off at white America. In Christianity we usually talk about sinfulness as being a matter of the human heart. It is hard to conclude otherwise, looking at the Gospels where Christ reveals his personality as someone poignantly aware of what is inside the human heart. What is deep inside us becomes the material for the relationship with God.

The "Wrightian Shift," as I call it, makes the social issue the priority rather than what only God sees within us. What happens socially matters more than what individuals do or harbor in their hearts. The converse to this is that no matter what offense a black man has done, because of the history of his race, he could never as an individual merit Hell. For white people, that was another matter.

How Americans will be persuaded to accept the murder of fellow citizens

A 2011 guest, a Jewish New Yorker, on the *Glenn Beck Program* offered an interesting parallel. The man was a Jewish New Yorker. He explained how people in the Third Reich could come to accept the atrocities of murdering millions of European Jews. He draws a parallel between the early events in Germany and what has been happening in the United States. Early on, the German people began to accept the absence (i.e. murder) of the most extreme elements of society: the gypsies, the homosexuals, the mentally disabled. Silence over these seemingly less important, less relevant elements of society created a barrier to future opposition to the National Socialist extermination of Jews. How could they be inclined to object to the removal of their neighbors when they had already accepted the extermination of lesser people

Pro-Choice as a prelude to the ovens

The parallel with the progressive agenda is in the realm of thought

There has to be a willingness to accept a certain kind of illogical thinking in advancing the progressive changes, and that illogicality starts with the statements of pro-choice. Why is it illogical?

"Pro-choice" is like saying, "I'm for preferring." You would then ask, "preferring what?"

In pro-choice, the preference is to terminate a life, but one has difficulty stating this and regresses to the incomplete, illogical expression. It is precisely these inroads taken into logical structure of thought that will make it more difficult to reject what will come later. Simply put, faulty logic will eliminate the freedom of speech and freedom of religion, and will facilitate persecution of Americans for various forms of expression. Make no mistake about it: according to our scenario, in Obama's second term, thousands of Americans will be carted off to prisons and specially constructed mental health facilities without a trial of any kind. All this will be done for "the good of the people." We can't have a few standing in the way of what's being done for the rest of us. This has been the ubiquitous hallmark of every progressive political movement.

But what is the actual crime of the few?

Psychiatry in Obama Two.

For decades political correctness has been a topic of jokes, but in Obama Two it will develop into full-blown criminal action, a fall-out from the courts of the European Union. Political correctness will be insidiously interwoven with hate speech and criticism of the government, offenses punishable by fine and imprisonment. This scenario forecasts that changes in psychiatry will expedite the progressive agenda by eliminating individual dissent. This, of course, has been done by progressive regimes in the past.

Vladimir Bukovsky was one of the first to expose the Soviet Union's use of psychiatric imprisonment of political prisoners. The Russian writer and neurophysiologist is a leading member of the Soviet dissident movement of the 1960s and 1970s. Bukovsky was sentenced to twelve years in a variety of Soviet institutions, including prisons, labor camps, and forced-treatment psychiatric hospitals known as *psikhushkas*. These hospitals were used by the government as special prisons and served as an excellent method of enforcing political censorship.

Currently in the United States, the *Diagnostic and Statistical Manual* (DSM), a classification and treatment manual for psychiatric illnesses is in the process of being updated and will be known as the DSM-V once finished. Psychiatry is a branch of medicine that is especially susceptible to political pressure, and that a state of flux currently prevails in the compilation of the DSM-V comes as no surprise. The 2012 debate on the DSM includes controversy concerning the inclusion of transgender persons. It appears that there is considerable disagreement about this even in the transgender community itself.

Benedict Carey of the *New York Times* reports that "Dr. Jack Drescher, a New York psychoanalyst and member of the sexual disorders work group, said that, in some ways, the gender identity debate echoed efforts to remove homosexuality from the manual in the 1970s."

This '70s revision of homosexuality in the DSM received a great deal of criticism. Some claimed that the updaters of the manual succumbed to political pressure. And it is not unreasonable to expect that Political pressure may again be seen in the revised DSM, an outcome that's especially likely in view of the fact that the current administration has gained extensive control over the entire health care system.

With respect to the European Union, Bukovsky suggests that the *psikhushkas* may make a comeback. Just as Stalin progressives installed special psychiatric prisons in the USSR, the Obama progressives may be expected to do the same with dissidents in United States. Bukovsky already see signs of it.

The crime of the few

When we take out the intimate relationship between God and man, in which God alone can look into human hearts, then we can put into the hearts of our fellow human beings whatever we want.

Progressives use the dynamics of deep-seated racial hatred and taking a page from the Freudian playbook, in that they can claim it's the underlying motivation of anything they wish. We have already seen this concept of thought judgment. In convicting someone of a hate crime, for example, the subject is found guilty for what was in his head, as decided by the courts. In the Fox scandal, progressives strive to conclude that Murdoch must have been personally involved in phone hacking because the intent was present in his mind all along.

In developing thought control, the progressive agenda will rely on the important area of design control, the subject of our next chapter.

CHAPTER 18

Design

In September of 2011 a gentleman named "Chris" sat before the American TV audience and announced his reason for buying Ford: "I was going to buy from a manufacturer that's standing on their own: win, lose, or draw. That's what America is about is taking the chance to succeed and understanding when you fail that you gotta pick yourself up and go back to work."

Analysis

The first thing we can say is that there is little doubt that this Ford ad leveled a blow against the White House, slamming the Obama administration's bailout of the auto industry and the philosophy behind it. Now, put yourself in the place of automakers GM and Chrysler. Out of Detroit's "Big Three," Ford was the only company that didn't accept bailout dollars from the federal government. (Of course, they have taken government funds in the past.) What does that say about you if you are one of the Big Three that *did* take bailout money—you are unable to stand on your own, unable to pick yourself up and go back to work, unable to be "what America is [all] about."

A couple of things happened after this ad:

The ad was taken off the air and removed from YouTube, where it had also been running.

Conservative blog *The Hill* reported the ad gone from both TV stations and YouTube. *The Hill* further reported that a call was place by the White House to the Ford Motor Corp.

The *Media Matters* blog charged that the facts were misrepresented in conservative media. As a rule *Media Matters* slants their posts toward supporting the Obama administration and attacks blogs and websites unfavorable to Obama or typical leftist causes.

Political orientation determines how one looks at the Ford ad controversy:

Right: The ad disappeared from TV stations.

Left: Ford claims the ad ran its scheduled course and was followed by another already scheduled.

Right: The ad was pulled off YouTube.

Left: It was reinstated.

Right: The White House pressured Ford into removing the ad.

Left: Ford social media director Scott Monty tweets, "We did not pull the ad under pressure."

Daniel Howes, a conservative columnist for the *Detroit News*, was the first to report that Ford decided to pull the ad after a call from the White House. He did not say that the administration had asked specifically for the ad to be pulled and quoted an industry source that said that the automaker was not pressured.

Media Matters is correct. Except for the pulling the ad off YouTube (which may well have been a snafu by some lower-level worker), there is no evidence the government pressured Ford. Is it a problem that the White House called Ford after a they ran a somewhat critical ad? I don't know. How typical is it that the White House calls a major auto company? Maybe it happens a lot.

However, the American media and a good percentage of the public wasn't ready to bury its suspicions. The Obama administration has been far from open about its dealings. Fear lingers that any government may control the media for its own purposes, sometimes even becoming outright oppressive. We have seen it before.

Government and art

Art has been used to support government goals. The power of art, in combination with the suppression of free speech or a free press, has been used as a tool by authoritarian governments to control their citizens. The Mussolini regime, for example, had an authoritarian control over the media (yet Italian cinema still came out with some notable film classics during this period). During any war both sides employ propaganda; both mobilize the art community.

The prolific anti-Bush art that emerged pre-2008 is an example of art being used in opposition to a government administration. Graphic designer Milton Glaser (of the "I-heart-New York" fame) produced anti-Bush buttons for "The Nation." The *LA Times* sported a cover image of George W. Bush as a bloodthirsty vampire.

But something unusual has happened with art in the Obama administration. As Nick Gillespie reports in April 2009 on reason.com, "the art community has responded to the Obama administration's contradictions, hypocrisies, and distortions with near total silence." The only exception appears to be the anonymous Obama "Joker" posters that have been appearing in Los Angeles.

How did journalists and art reviewers respond to this creative challenge to the Obama administration? With racial accusations: "The Joker white-face imposed on Obama's visage has a sort of malicious, racist, Jim Crow quality to it."

Gillespie asks, "Why would any artist who hopes to have (or keep) a career create images that criticize the president when both journalists and art reviewers make such irrational comments?"

The call to the 75

"This is just the beginning. This is the first telephone call of a *brand new* conversation. We are just now learning how to really bring this community together to speak *with* the government. What that looks like legally?…bear with us as we learn the language so that we can speak to each other safely…"

The above is an extract from a conference call that took place on August 10 2011. Emboldened by the art communities' uncritical embracement of Barack Obama, the White House—together with the National Endowment for the Arts (NEA), and the president's nationwide campaign for all citizens' service, United We Serve—attempted to recruit selective creative talent to form favorable public response to progressive changes. Patrick Courrielche revealed the nature the conference call that included the above quote. Specifically the targeted group was to create an amenable environment for accommodation of the administration's position on key issues. This would include healthcare, energy, and the environment—all subjects of intense national debate.

Parties involved

- **Yosi Sergant**, the director of communications for the National Endowment for the Arts

- **Buffy Wicks,** deputy director of the White House Office of Public Engagement

- **Nell Abernathy,** director of outreach for United We Serve;

- **Thomas Bates**, vice president of Civic Engagement for Rock the Vote

- **Michael Skolnik**, political director for Russell Simmons

The telecon with the weight of the White House advocating for creative propaganda was made public. Faced with the revelation of their efforts to recruit artists for their political ends, the administration was in a bind. Since they couldn't spin it, they had to deny that the call was ever made. However, it wasn't long before the e-mails were produced indicating both White House and NEA involvement.

NEA funds

That the NEA participated in such a frank political effort was disturbing to many. In 1965 the NEA was established to increase access to the arts and support education in that realm. Networking for political propaganda is a role completely unauthorized for the organization

While it's true that artists threw themselves into the 2008 election with great excitement and enthusiasm, this NEA-sanctioned recruitment is an entirely different matter. It's an attempt to manufacture expression on behalf of the government agenda. Clearly the issues presented in the teleconference were subject to intense political debate in the legislature. Doesn't the legislature represent the people?

Some artists considered it a dangerous step for a government-sponsored art program to take a position on contested issues. Other artists still favoring Obama felt it was no big deal since they would be promoting the administration's reelection anyway. To those, Courrielche warns, "What if opponents were to do the same thing; do you want to empower any government like that?"

Scenario—control of media talent

We have already mentioned that it is the goal of progressives to create a culture that is in many ways foreign to American traditions, to create a state that many Americans will find repugnant. Consider the following issues that could easily be subject to artistic developments:

- Sexual education for the young

- Limitation of conscience exemption

- Disposition to health-care reform measures

- Acceptance of increased taxation

- Government intimidation

We have only to refer to the Jaffee Memorandum, the suggested goals offered by Planned Parenthood—which Obama has consistently supported—to find an agenda for using excessive propaganda to reengineer American society.

Penalty for dissident artists

The ever-present coercion factor in the progressive agenda will come into play in the mobilization of artist participation. All Americans must serve, and because the NEA is a major funder of arts—and also attracts matching funds—one can expect that lack of participation in the agenda will mean a lack of funding for those young developing artists.

There is little doubt the progressive government will develop a political test for artists. Consider how the Obama administration funds his much praised community music programs listed on the website that proclaims Obama's achievements. But Obama didn't simply provide funds to the community and open an opportunity for all musicians interested in teaching music to youth. Rather the funding went specifically to government-created programs. The concept is chilling: only federal-government-sanctioned providers teach music to little children.

> *This is just the beginning. This is the first telephone call of a brand new conversation. We are just now learning how to really bring this community together to speak with the government. What that looks like legally?…bear with us as we learn the language so that we can speak to each other safely…*

CHAPTER 19

Energy Control

In a biology class at the University of Hawaii, a professor has just completed a drawing on the board. It was one of those exponential curves that represented the growth of bacteria in the presence of an abundance of sugar. As he speaks, he traces his hand along the smooth curve that rises increasingly steeper with each second of time. He suddenly turns and asks, "Looking at this, does anyone in this room doubt that bacteria are a slave to energy?"

No one answers.

Then he quickly follows with another question. "What other organism is a slave to energy?"

The class is still surprised by the abruptness of this sudden Socratic diversion from the usual lecturing at this hour of the morning. They remain silent.

The professor persists, searching the room for a reply. "Who else is a slave to energy? Who else?"

The room remains quiet. Suddenly he gives the response he is looking for; it comes hissing between his teeth: "Humans! Man! Man is a slave to energy!"

That scene from the '60s college experience stuck in my mind. Early on I couldn't understand the connection between the observation of energy use and the emotion, the contempt that the professor had for his own species. The explanation lies in the progressive perception of the connection between human population and energy resources. Available energy underpins population growth. Control one, you control the other.

You will never understand the energy policies of the Obama administration unless you put it together with the goal of global contraception.

The pragmatic fear of overpopulation fits nicely with the need to control energy. I refer to it as the *Columbine thesis*. Things are getting worse. There are too many people on the planet. I'm too many people; you're too many. Something's got to be done. You can be eliminated; I can be eliminated.

To learn how the Obama administration plans to handle things, we have simply to refer to the Jaffee Memo discussed in more detail below. Obama has already stated that under his plan "…the costs of energy would skyrocket." Some people look at the video in which he said that and are dumbfounded. Why would the president want people to struggle even more to pay utility bills? But an understanding of the above energy-population relationship explains this statement nicely. Again notice that the element of coercion is always integral to any Obama strategy: if the people are unwilling to control population, the government will enforce it through other means.

Our energy use and production

Only China surpasses the United States in energy consumption. Most of our energy is derived from fossil fuels: 37 percent from petroleum, 21 percent from coal, and 25 percent from natural gas. Nuclear power supplies 9 percent.

There has been a lot of discussion on renewable energy, which includes hydroelectric dams, wind power, geothermal power, and solar energy. This supplied only 8 percent of our energy in 2011. While renewable energy is desirable, it takes a great deal of creativity to make it a practical source of energy. It is one thing to mandate it; delivering on it is an entirely different matter.

Since we consume energy faster than we produce it, we have to rely on imports. It's important to note that if energy costs go up, so does the price of everything else. Transportation, food, clothing costs will certainly rise. Just looking at China, we can see a clear relation between available energy and GDP. Business expansion and employment are intimately related to the availability of energy.

So what has the administration done so far in Obama One to advance control of energy? Supporters mostly refer to breakthrough regulations affecting fuel efficiency. This requires doubling current standards by 2015. How Obama knows that this is possible with available technology is a mystery, but if the goal is not met there will likely be regulatory fines.

In the July 2011 issue of *LA Times,* Michael Brune notes that "Environmentalists worked hard to help Barack Obama win the presidency. Three years later, many of us are disappointed with the administration's environmental record. Although headlines proclaiming that Al Gore "condemned," "blasted" or "slammed" the president in his recent *Rolling Stone* essay were exaggerated, there's no skirting the administration's failure to take bold action on protecting our communities, rivers, lakes, oceans, wild lands, air and climate."

There is no doubt however that the president was "condemned, blasted, or slammed" by his critics in another matter—that of Solyndra.

The Solyndra scandal

Barack Obama's pilot into green stimulus has been called "an extravagant display of cronyism at its best." It started with an award of 535 million taxpayer dollars to a green energy company called Solyndra, in an effort to create green jobs. Critics claim this loan guarantee was a smokescreen for a payoff to a big-time Democrat and Obama donor, George Kaiser, who holds the largest stake in Solyndra. However, as *Media Matters* pointed out, Republican supporters also had a stake in the company. The end result was bankruptcy, the laying off 1,100 employees, and a $535 million loss; a congressional investigation was launched.

Concern for green energy needs often leads to unrealistic responses. The following blog posting is typical:

> It is possible to re-engineer the whole planet away from using fossil fuels and fracking up the environment. It needs far sighted investment into alternatives, which would create jobs and industry in various types of energy.

The problem is investments don't create jobs. Now, when I say that, people respond with, "You're crazy; of course it does." Well, yes, it certainly creates jobs for some scientists and engineering people if that's what you mean, but if you mean the kinds of jobs that we associate with the employment figures we monitor almost daily, we would have to say that investment alone will not create those figures. What do you need to create jobs?

You need a product.

To create a product, you have to think of the men and women that will be using the product and how it will be integrated in their work or their lives. That's the kind of thinking that makes for a successful product. That requires knowledge of the marketplace, intelligence, and creativity. Being driven by an ideology alone will not suffice.

Not long ago I took an open house tour of my son's place of employment, a successful electrical equipment manufacturer called S&C, a recipient of TARP funding for the green energy sector. As I looked at the various demonstrations, I found myself completely lost in an extraordinary display of the most complicated equipment. Despite a flurry of friendly explanations from everyone, I had no idea what I was looking at or what the equipment was for. However, taking a break, I happened to come across a photographic display of the history of S&C.

The company's first product was a fuse, which in those early days of the twentieth century was a new concept. Growing

American populations started living in larger cities, like Chicago, where multistory apartment buildings were built and electricity introduced in apartments. With only a simple wiring scheme, the conduits would frequently overheat, causing disastrous fires. To solve this problem, the S&C founders Edmund O. Schweitzer and Nocholas J. Conrad developed a fuse, a device that would shut off electrical flow if overheating occurred.

In looking at the photographs revealing the various steps to put this invention on the market, I was struck by the dedication the founders exhibited in making sure that the products would fit into the needs of the potential customers. Their product was tested in all kinds of weather before coming onto the market. One of the founders actually stayed on his job at Edison Electric for seven years after production began, and other employees had been hired just to make sure that there would be enough cash flow available to help the company become a success. How different things were at Solyndra.

Lindsey Eastburn, former Solyndra engineer, told the *Washington Post*, "After we got the loan guarantee, they were just spending money left and right...Because we were doing well, nobody cared. Because of that infusion of money, it made people sloppy."

Solyndra may have actually had a competitive product that yielded more electricity with its photovoltaic system compared with conventional rooftop solar panels. The problem came in integrating production, inventory supply, and customer demand.

Does solar power work?

Solar power, although pricey, is touted as one of the cleanest methods of energy production around. The claim is that solar panels simply convert the energy of the sun into energy mankind can use, and there are no harmful byproducts or threats to the environment. However, a recent report appearing in the *LA Times* questions this.

To begin with, manufacturing the solar panels themselves requires a whopping dose of fossil fuels. Add to this a disposal problem associated with byproducts of mercury and chromium. The installation of solar panels requires use of PVC and a variety of glues. Asia is one of the leading manufacturers of solar panels, and countries there are now beginning to confront disposal problems associated with all the toxins used in the creation of the product. These problems are not insoluble, but they will certainly require attention before we can claim solar panel power has no impact on the environment.

Does the market need to be controlled?

Perhaps the most disturbing thing about the Solyndra controversy was Obama's reaction to the company's demise. His comments indicated that the problem with Solyndra had to do with the improper response of the market. The facts contradict this assessment. Solyndra did, in fact, have orders for solar panels, but their production and delivery schedule couldn't keep up with competitors. But the president's comments betray the coercive undertones behind a progressive environmental agenda.

Energy futuring for Obama Two.

How will energy play into our scenario for the second Obama administration? Consider the following attack truths:

Truth One   Our planet appears affected by energy use.
Truth Two   Humans are wasteful in energy utilization.
Truth Three We would be better off if alternative sources of energy were available.

We can expect the administration to develop coercive strategy that will couple energy and environmental measures with reproductive control objectives. We predict increased regulation and penalty fines on energy-related businesses. The program will involve the recruitment of youth to form a civilian force trained in green technology enforcement. We predict restriction on business growth, increased unemployment, and a substantial decrease in GDP.

Before leaving the topic of energy control, I should point out the intricate relationship between energy and population control alluded to at the beginning of the chapter. One will never understand the Obama progressive energy policy unless one puts it together with population control through enhanced contraception, widespread abortion at all stages, and the encouragement of homosexuality and independent female habitation. These are all closely integrated in the Obama progressive ideology affecting energy. Control energy flow, as Obama did, by prohibiting it on federal lands, and one control's human procreation. As progressives see it, the relationship between population and energy exhibits a fundamental socio-biological principle.

Knowing this, one can appreciate what a tremendous asset in Obama's plan for energy control are the activities of Planned Parenthood, a topic discussed in the next chapter.

CHAPTER 20

Population impact

Going into 2012 the American people will be ideologically divided as evidenced by the election results. The division at that time will be between pro government-restraint conservatives and liberals desirous of increased government funding, especially if it's tied to the interests of the neglected segment of the US population.

The second term will introduce new stressors. The people will see an even greater increase in taxes starting in 2013. They will see new financial burdens in the form of fines associated with personal and family energy use as well as failure to comply with new progressive acts. Up will go the cost of everything they buy. Ever-growing government regulations will also level fines on businesses, thereby reducing employment and individual salaries. The smaller midsized business will be less able to pay and will struggle to survive. As Obama promised, under the progressive plan energy costs will skyrocket and with it the affordability of everything else.

After 2013, however, the division of the American public will fall along an entirely different fault line. On one side will be the more privileged, who feel the yield from the progressive plan is worth the financial burdens, and on the other side will those who don't like the idea because they're not "invited in" to enjoy any of the benefits. The number of those unconvinced of progressive benefits will approach 70 percent by 2018 as will the number in the non-privileged subject classes.

Termination of townships

If you live in a smaller town or know someone who does you may see the entity disappear. It will become a trend. As the scenario time-line approaches 2016 an increasing number of smaller townships will become extinct.

A slow economy will not be their only financial problem. Whopping unfunded pension liabilities will play a huge role. By the middle of 2012, townships all across America will have already faced considerable municipal worker layoff schedules. The socio-economic structure of many non-urban Americans will change radically giving rise to cultural instability in this population.

Going after revenue through an increase in traffic fines using enhanced police activity will make towns less attractive to the surrounding suburban market and hasten their demise. If you're a Mayor and you ticket a consumer in your township they'll never come back. Why should they when there are so many other suburban centers just as close? Why risk getting strapped with an unreasonable fine like a $100 citation for turning right on a red light when no traffic is in sight? Investing in traffic photo enforcement will be a virtual death sentence for smaller towns. Repeat visitors will get wise and shop elsewhere; only folks who stray or get lost will venture in. Providers of this equipment are already considering asking for payment in full before shipping to desperate smaller governments.

Many towns will eventually succumb to bankruptcy, consolidation with other municipalities, or federal control. Pensions for the retired? Forget about it.

Employment

Most economic forecasts call for a slow, steady improvement of the economy. What kind of changes can we expect to see in the workplace in Obama Two?

"I love my job, but love my life more." This is the kind of expression we can expect to hear a lot as the new Gen Y comes onto the scene.

Definition: Gen Y is usually defined by those workers born between 1980 and 2000.

Gen Yers come loaded with aspirations and appear to have a much greater tendency to follow their dreams than older workers have. Turnover in the Gen Y set is higher than in previous generations: 34 percent of employers admit that the turnover rate rose with improvement of employment opportunities between 2009 and 2010. Employers will be expected to mobilize workplace enhancements to hold on to employees they want.

Older workers with four or more years of employment difficulties may feel forced to make adaptations. As the employment picture worsens for many, the percentage rate for the unemployed becomes less meaningful. It doesn't account for the modifications, for individual economic responses, including dropping out of conventional employment avenues. This may entail family consolidation of housing and food resources, part-time employment and various degrees of underemployment. Individual aspirations submerge without any hope of fulfillment. The goal: survive and pay taxes.

Government workers

Government employment will become an increasingly desirable vocation in Obama's second term. Increased status, desirable benefits, including student loan forgiveness—all these will cause the swelling of the ranks of federal workers by the more fortunate.

Actually the financial cushion for federal workers has been generously increasing since 2005, but the Obama administration still gave it a boost: Government employees earning $150,000 or more doubled since June 2009. In 2005 the Department of Defense had 9 civilians earning $175,000 or greater. The number went from 9 to 214 when Obama took office. In June of 2010 it leapt to 994.

There are, of course, some economists that will produce studies showing that government workers get paid less than their civilian counterparts, but these are misleading. For example, a distinction should be made between federal and nonfederal government employees. If you look at a position, say a microbiologist working for some government agency, and compare that salary to a microbiologist working in a cutting-edge high-tech firm, then yes, there will be a difference. Put together enough of those situations, and you will skew the statistics. Another flaw with the study is looking at salaries and comparing educational backgrounds of government and nongovernment workers. You could have a better educated government worker doing the same job and getting the same pay as a nongovernment worker. But does that extra education on the resume have anything to do with the job requirements? Or does it just reflect a more privileged background? If economists wanted to do an honest study, they would look at federal employees versus civilians. They would look at starting pay and benefits for beginning civilian workers and compare them with what someone entering a government position can expect. The difference is in favor of the federal employee, and it is growing.

The disparity in employment benefits between most of the private sector on the one hand, and the government and politically important labor unions on the other will gradually give rise to a privileged class.

The progressive changes in the workplace

Using the Jaffe Memorandum as a guide you will see

- Mandated racial diversity in every department of every organization.

- Explicit manifestations of homosexuality in the workplace

- Encouragement of women to work with fewer child care options available except for politically sensitive minority settings.

Following the recommendations from Planned Parenthood, government control measures will discourage pregnancy coverage in insurance plans. We will see a reduction or elimination of paid maternity leave.

Now there is some conflict between the above statements and what Americans are told to expect from the new health care bill. Whereas currently many insurance plans do not offer pregnancy coverage, the Obama administration plan mandates it for all insurers. Surely this goes against our progressive forecast.

The key thing to note about the Obama care is that there is uncertainty in funding it. On paper, the program relies on the elimination of fraud and increased efficiency in the delivery of care. (Most economists doubt the likelihood of this unprecedented view of eliminating costs.) Pregnancy costs are a huge financial expense of any insurance plan. Not everyone is going to want pregnancy coverage, and as costs skyrocket there will be agitation between those who need pregnancy coverage and those who don't—another Alinsky provision of divisiveness.

"People having children are going to make the rest of us pay for it. Health care costs enough as it is. It isn't fair." This will be the cry that supports the impetus not only for the curtailment of pregnancy benefits but also for another government action that will follow: the selective right to conceive, an element in the Jaffee Memorandum for Planned Parenthood.

Planned Parenthood Federation of America

The most merciful thing that the large family does to one of its infant members is to kill it... All our problems are the result of over breeding among the working class. —Margaret Sanger, founder of Planned Parenthood

We must resolutely oppose...inundation of those nonwhite...regions inhabited by really inferior races." —Lothrop Stoddard, member of the board of directors of Sanger's foundation

If ever there was an excellent example of the use of the Alinsky attack truth to advance deceit, it would have to be Planned Parenthood. Today there are an extraordinary number of Americans who are totally ignorant both of the history of this organization and of its ultimate objectives affecting humankind. Many hasten to defend Planned Parenthood, especially while recalling past periods of their life when they may have been most grateful for benefits received, from "PP" such as contraceptives and health related services, like breast examinations. What they don't realize is that most of these benefits came from donations by parties other than Planned Parenthood. The gift, nonetheless, allows the benevolent image of the organization to prevail.

Steven W. Mosher of the Population Institute relates how in her 1922 book, *Pivot of Civilization*, Margaret Sanger "unabashedly calls for the extirpation of 'weeds...overrunning the human garden'; for the segregation of 'morons, misfits, and the maladjusted'; and for the sterilization of 'genetically inferior races.'"

Because of her association with contraception, Sanger has often been held up as a champion of women's rights. Nothing could be further from the truth. In her 1934 *Code to Stop Overproduction of Children,* Sanger decreed that "no woman shall have a legal right to bear a child without a permit...No permit shall be valid for more than one child."

From this perspective, and given the forecast of this scenario based on the Jaffe memoranda, one can see that law student Sandra Fluke's protest is properly regarded as the *avant garde* of the progressive assault on women's freedom of procreation. Phase one is to assure there is no resistance to contraception, even at *Real Katolique* institutions, such as Georgetown. The second phase, according to the Planned Parenthood memorandum, will be coercive regulation in accordance with Sanger's code.

Fluke's display would hardly convince millions of Chinese women that she expresses any concern for women's rights. Their plight under China's progressive rule received exposure, thanks to blind Chinese dissident Chen Guangcheng and his courageous study of the government-enforced birth control.

Mosher further relates what it was that brought about the renaming of Sanger's foundation as Planned Parenthood Federation of America. The original name "The American Birth Control League" suggested coercion. Mosher explains, "War with Germany, combined with lurid tales of how the Nazis were putting her theories about 'human weeds' and 'genetically inferior races' into practice, panicked Sanger into changing her organization's name and rhetoric."

Today people still speak of birth control with little realization that the word "control" meant not control by the individual but rather control by organizations like Planned Parenthood.

Our scenario forecasts rapid deployment of national militia to accomplish Obama/Progressive objectives. We predict a parallel will occur between the actions of the National Socialists in the Third Reich and that of the Jaffee/Pelosi/Progressives in Obama Two. Both regimes are fertile ground for progressive theories.

Sanger/National Socialists:	Control of Europe by Nazi forces.
Jaffee/Obama progressives:	Control of America in Next 2000 days.

In Obama's second term, the government will exploit any opportunity to sway public sentiment against human procreation. If you are the kind of person that feels there are too many people on the planet or that global problems are due to too many people, you have already bought into the Planned Parenthood agenda.

Rise of the *apparatchik*; Durbanism.

In Obama Two, as already noted, we will see the development of two important divisions within the American population.

Government and labor union officials will share a privileged status as the difference between the becomes increasingly blurred. Then there will be the rest of Americans.

There is a striking parallel between this new American dichotomy and that which developed in the Soviet Union. Combined government-union bureaucracy is, for all intents and purposes, a faithful representation of the Soviet *apparatchik,* which was comprised of the full-time professionals of the Communist Party. Like its Soviet counterpart, the American *apparatchik* makes a distinction between the privileges of the Party (government and union echelons) and the lot of the public. For the public, the Party members construct the various government programs, but the family members of the *apparatchik* enjoy many other benefits and privileges.

An excellent example of an American *apparatchik* would very likely be Dick Durban, a Democratic member of the US Senate. His background is relatively sparse in private enterprise experience except for the practice of law, preparatory for the election process. The mind-set of the *apparatchik,* which is founded on a lack of parity between the Party members and those served by their processes, can be seen in the matter of the Washington DC voucher controversy.

In 2004, a school voucher system was set up to help poor students in the horrific District of Columbia public school system. The vouchers would allow them to escape from DC public schools and attend private institutions. If you looked at the schools these students would have gone to without the voucher system, you would find that 92 percent of them were in need of improvement, corrective action, or restructuring. The five-year pilot program was the first federally funded program providing K–12 education grants. It had strong support from the black community. According to Washington editor Mike Lynch, "The help these families wanted most is help leaving government schools." The pilot study showed that the kids in the program outperformed the kids that were left behind.

Who didn't like the idea of these kids getting ahead? The American *apparatchik,* of course.

The Democratic Party receives support from the teachers union that, in general, opposes vouchers. (As do most Americans, according to surveys.) Democratic Mayor Vincent Gray complained that district-wide testing didn't show any advantage of the program. Of course that fails to take into account the much higher graduation rate of students in the program, which means they were more likely to be around for the testing in the first place. Ted Kennedy tried to keep the program from starting: "It takes funds from very needy public schools to send students to unaccountable private schools." Durban managed to eliminate the program by attaching an amendment to a 2009 spending bill.

Lesson from DC voucher controversy

The biggest obstacle to better education for individual minority students: Teachers Unions. Notice what happened here. Kids received a far better education than they otherwise would have. The voucher solved the problem of the inferior DC system *in the case of these students*, not for everyone, but it did for this group. But note, once again, that the progressives do not really want to solve problems, per se. They want to solve them in accordance with an ideology which, in this case, is the preservation of the privilege of the party to attend excellent schools and the relegation of the public to inferior educational programs.

The kids escaped the progressive program; the infants escaped the abortion. They both need to learn their place in the progressive scheme of things.

But the kids who were already in the program got a lucky break. Sidwell Friends is one of Washington's best private schools. It's not surprising that President Barack Obama sends his daughters to attend Sidwell, and it so happened that a few of their classmates are beneficiaries of the DC voucher program. (Presumably government funding via a paycheck pays for the faire of the President's children as well.) Rather than have his daughters see the children dragged out of their classes simply because they were poor, Obama stepped in and agreed to allow students currently enrolled to graduate. But the program could no longer accept new applicants. No more invasion of the *apparatchik* privileges.

Later development: GOP House Speaker Boehner and Democratic Senator Lieberman supported a bill to restore the program.

Under the progressive rule of Obama Two, we can expect to find an extraordinary gap develop between the privileged government class and that of the general public, increasingly controlled by the various agencies that will shortly develop.

Smaller class segments

In addition to the government-Party *apparatchik*, the second Obama administration will see the development of certain other classes, but most of these will be temporary, ending by 2018.

Minorities will be recipients of special treatment, such as preferential admission of blacks to medical colleges and government employment opportunities for other minorities. Minorities represented by certain community organizations will be exempt from debt obligations, such as home mortgages, or will see them greatly diminished. This will be spearheaded by protests along the lines of Occupy Wall Street.

Consider how this new change in debt obligations comes about. First, we have the deplorable picture of big banks and other mortgage holders refusing to negotiate with financially strapped minority homeowners struggling to prevent foreclosure and eviction from their homes. This is no doubt distressing.

Community groups and segments from Occupy Wall Street become involved, staging Alinsky-style protests at home sites and lender sites. The financial institutions capitulate.

Note that, here again, we have community nonprofit control of private enterprise. In fact, George Soros-backed organizations have taken out public ads asking for young people who would care to train as "bank terrorists."

The unrepresented customer base of these financial institutions will have to cover any financial loss that results from bank terrorism concessions. This will add to the developing pressures that will collapse the credit market.

The "illegal" immigrant population will form another class that will be developed as they enter an amnesty program. All of the above subclasses will be temporary. By 2018, they and the other subclasses will have been absorbed into either the government workers or the general public.

Labor unions

Americans live in a country where individuals can be deprived of their property without any right of appeal. It happens every day. It's called collective bargaining agreements with public employee unions.

There is no doubt that organized labor will be an important factor in the transformation of American society in Obama Two. Organized labor has gained substantial inroads into the American power structure, and its political and economic influence is growing. Service Employees International Union (SEIU), a public employee union, spent $28 million supporting Barack Obama in the 2008 presidential election, making it the "organization that spent the most to help Barack Obama get elected president." Even with a decline in the number of members, the amount of revenue received by unions has grown to over 10 billion.

The Alinsky attack truth

Notice that labor unions also develop from the Alinsky attack truth. The truth is that many employers have engaged in unfair, if not inhuman, labor practices in the past, and not a few of them would continue to do so were it not for organized labor.

Unions have no limits on spending to support candidates and members can't object.

However, union influence has allowed organized labor to enjoy a barrage of special legal privileges and immunities. The Federal Campaign Act exempts unions from limitations on campaign contributions and even certain reporting requirements. Unions can spend unlimited amounts to communicate with members and their families in order to support or oppose candidates for federal office, and they need not report these expenditures. All they have to do is send it in a publication chock-full of other union stuff.

Suppose you're a union member employee who finds himself in opposition to union political candidates or goals. In most cases that's tough luck. Employees are often powerless to prevent unions from funding candidates or goals they don't agree with.

Court rulings okay violence

Probably one of the most frightening aspects of government-sanctioned union privileges is the ability to perpetrate violence without any legal liability. Imagine what this means. For example you are in a situation where you become subject to violence against you as an individual and the government will take no action to assist you. That's basically the kind of situation that you're looking at here. How could this be possible? The situation developed over several years. One can look at the Supreme Court decision of *US vs. Emmons*, where union members fired rifles at three utility company transformers, drained the oil from another, and blew up an entire company substation. The court ruled there was no liability on the part of the labor union. Some legal experts claim the labor violence incidents are really too small in number to cause real concern. They argue that there is no need for special legislation. However, examples of union violence are not hard to find.

Take, for instance, the situation of John King, a Toledo Ohio operator of a nonunion electrical contracting business. With twenty-five employees, King is one of the largest electrical contractors in the area. King found himself facing numerous threats, legal battles, and vandalism stemming from union resentment; his employees were the subject of verbal abuse by union thugs. Then came the recession. A non-union contractor, King's business happened to be doing well at a time when unions in the construction industry were suffering. Union backlash reached a climax in August 2011 when a union member tried to kill him in his own home.

Then we come across the possible facilitation of Union thuggery by the Obama administration

During his election campaign, Barack Obama promised he would ban the use of permanent replacement workers as a favor to unions. However, even with control of both houses, he failed to get the legislation through Congress. To compensate for this, Obama and company developed a more sinister strategy: **develop hit lists of individuals to be targeted by unions.** Since he couldn't fulfill a promise with the legislature, due to his lack of leadership ability, Obama would achieve it through the executive branch.

President Obama's union appointees in the Department of Labor are in the process of doing just this. Information regarding replacement workers, including details of home addresses and phone numbers, will be collected, posted, and made public on the Departments of Labor's website for anyone to see. **Obama wants to give unions a "ready-made 'scab' list" of people to target—at their homes and school districts where their children attend.**

There have been several attempts by Republicans in Congress to pass a "freedom from union violence" act, but so far efforts have been unsuccessful due to union control of Democratic Congressmen.

Collective bargaining

Franklin Delano Roosevelt was a champion of collective bargaining for the private sector. However, when it came to government employees, he expressed nothing but staunch opposition to collective bargaining. Why?

Well, consider that the federal employees are essentially working for the whole people; their employers are the general public. What does it mean if an administrator is bargaining with the union in a bilateral agreement when we already have a system for the American people to express their consent? It's called Congress, the place where representatives go to pass new laws.

Now the argument here is that government administrators cannot bind voters to rules and still be in conformity with their constitutional way of life. That's because the voters are not represented in the collective agreement; they are represented in Congress. and if the administrator could bind voters to the collective bargaining rules, that would mean that legislation affecting labor agreements could never be enacted by the people, even if it were necessary to reject collective agreements to prevent insolvency.

Let's consider the legal aspect of this. We mentioned before that individuals, according to our law, cannot be deprived of property or other rights without having some kind of individual appeal. In the private sector, shareholders can have representatives, who may vote to decrease their shares to increase corporate revenue. However, if they don't like it, investors can go can sell their shares or trade them for a new company.

Public citizens are not in the same situation. If you are going to negotiate a contract authorizing increased expenditures to union members, that increased income will have to come by way of increased taxation, and increased taxation means public citizens are, in fact, deprived of their personal income. That is essentially being deprived of property without recourse.

The government and SEIU

Labor unions have benefited from their intimate relationship with government. Take a look at the scheme:

1. The government gets revenues from taxpayers.
2. The union-paid lobbyists make campaign donations to politicians.
3. The politicians in office promise to spend taxpayer revenue on public works projects in exchange for campaign donations.
4. The revenue from the public works projects provides profit for more union contractors.
5. The union contractors support the lobbyists, who will then influence legislation to increase public works projects.

And on and on it goes.

As a favor to public service unions, the government collects funds from workers' paychecks.

Invasiveness of unions

Government increasingly allows unions to leach off of all payments going to government beneficiaries and even families caring for mental patients, in the name of providing increased benefits.

For example, using a scandalous mail-balloting campaign, the unions in Michigan created a $3.7 million revenue source in union dues from 40,000 day care workers in the state; most were surprised to find themselves unionized without their consent.

And if you think that's bad, consider this headline from NetRightDaily.com: **Outrage of the Day—SEIU Stealing from Cerebral Palsy Patients**. Rebecca DiFede provides the details: "In a disgusting display of greed a defunded quasi-government organization in Michigan known as the Michigan Quality Community

161

Care Council (MQC3), with the help of the Service Employees International Union (SEIU), found a way to dupe parents of sick children into giving them some of their much needed healthcare stipend. These tyrants reclassified thousands of parents receiving Medicare for the care of their adult children with cerebral palsy as care givers, thereby forcing them to join the SEIU and pay dues."

Scenario with union intervention

All this tells us that the country is currently powerless to deal with union organization. In fact it could easily be argued that we are governed by a triumvirate instead of a republic, where a single man acts as chief executive in name only. As details become known with time, Obama might have trouble claiming his a role as the first black president in American History. A review may well show that he wasn't acting as a president at all. The Obama administration will emerge as the first American triumvirate: George Soros providing the brains and the money; Andy Sterns, the muscle; and Obama, the bravado and image.

Tax liability

Even if Obama wasn't elected for a second term, Americans would have to endure increased tax liability.

Why?

Because we have an enormous debt that requires servicing. Dollars taken to pay interest on the debt must be taken from funds normally available for all the activities we associate with government administration. The government could, of course, simply print new money, but during the Obama's second term, China and other holders of US debt will put a restraint on that process with threats of dumping US Treasury debentures on the market.

Moreover, the government can expect a decrease in revenue from other sources as more business enterprises imitate General Electric and pay less as they create unrepatriated profits. They merely have to make payments to the progressive party.

"Pay fair share, you rich slobs" can never be a way to solve revenue needs. What happens if you tax wealthy citizens' assets? They move them offshore. Revenue? Ditto. Even if you took all the revenue from the rich, you still wouldn't have enough to significantly offset the debt burden. Obama knows this. His only purpose in raising the "fair share" issue was to create class resentment for Alinsky exploitation. Obama's party was in control of both houses of legislature for two years; he could have easily put "tax the rich" legislation in place, but he didn't even try.

Americans will also find themselves strapped with financial pressures from health care insurance premiums and penalties from energy law violation. Plus, the progressive party will integrate the reforms advanced by the Jaffe Memo into tax provisions. Modifications of tax liabilities will include the following:

- Marriage tax—tax for married people will be more than for single taxpayers.

- Child tax—additional taxes will be instituted for families with more than two children in school.

For the first time, a large number of Americans will find themselves in arrears, unable to pay taxes. Some fines will be payable in the long term, but others will require more immediate payment. As government liability increases, many will soon realize they will never be able to get caught up.

Something happens to people in these circumstances. Most consider it un-American not to pay their taxes, and responsible citizens tend to blame themselves. Some will be lost, incapable of understanding why they are unable to "pay their fair share." The threat of imprisonment, while initially unstated, begins to work on the mind. The onetime critics of government will become fearful, much less vocal. There will be no more Tea Party Protests by the end of 2015.

Enforcement

The infringement on individual family rights made important strides in the Bush administration when the census bureau empowered itself with the right to make unprecedented inquiries into home life. The legislature, with the single exception of Ron Paul, silently complied with the "necessary," although very likely unconstitutional, measure.

Obama's campaign promise to develop a civilian national force will begin in the summer of 2012. A much more aggressive effort will be made in the retaining of a youth political corps. The government-sponsored volunteer organizations will be earmarked as the enforcement arm for the new program to be developed in 2013. By the beginning of 2015, government regulation will invade all aspects of life. Noncompliant citizens will be paid a visit by a social police investigator and frequently fined or otherwise penalized.

Following the provisions of the Jaffe Planned Parenthood Memo, the Obama administration will enforce compulsory abortion, sterilization, and conception regulation for certain members of the population. Medical facilities will make family reproduction control the core of women's health.

Robertsian Oppression.

Perhaps no event was more helpful in achieving to progressive totalitarian control over the American people as a Supreme Court decision rendered by Chief Justice John Roberts in the June 2012 Affordable Care Act. There are profound similiarities between the Roberts action and the historical situation that developed in the course of the Hindenburg – Papen empowerments of Hitler. Like German Chancellor Franz von Papen, Roberts exhibited a naïve understanding of the individual he was about to transition into a dictator.

Papen received from Hitler a promise to govern in strict accordance with parliamentary procedure and to sustain the Weimar

Republic. In like manner Obama's oath as president required him to swear to uphold the U.S. Constitution.

Like Hitler, Obama received his launching point through legitimate measures. Once in power Hitler dissolved the Reichstag and called for new elections achieving victory by denying the opposition access to radio and free press. In The same way, Obama will eliminate the 2016 election and create a referendum to provide for the popular election results important in achieving supremacy. For both progressive parties, the Obama group and the Nazi party, a crisis will be used to expedite elections. In the case of the German Republic it was a fire in the Reichstag that led Hindenburg to suspend free speech and freedom of the press.

There is a direct relationship between the Roberts decision regarding the ability of the government to tax and the subsequent loss of free speech and the inevitable end to the American system of representative government. The mechanism is easy to follow.

Using government controlled healthcare as a model, the Obama administration will use tax as a penalty for failing to comply with administrative regulations. In Obama Two such regulations will extend to all levels of human existence. The financial constraints will put the majority of middle class in arrears with government obligations. Unable to achieve compliance, the masses will avoid any circumstances which could possibly lead to an investigation of their status. Fear of bullying by the ever present, ever-growing militia will have the effect of suppressing any open expression of opposition to government agendas.

Education

The Education Advancement Act of November 2014 will tie government-mandated programs to funding of both private and public schools. Sex education without parental notification or approval will be part of the compulsory education program for schoolchildren. Classroom sessions will stress the new picture of an ideal family with a limitation of the number of offspring to an approved number. Children will formulate this concept of normalcy and advance it among themselves and at home with parents. At first we will hear reports of the many parents that welcome the new educational practices. Those that object or feel concern about the child's attempt to educate parents will find themselves visited by government agencies and subject to a complete review of tax, energy, and health care insurance compliance. Fines and other measures for any and all violations will follow.

The Federally Insured Student Loan Program will be controlled by a progressive party unit that will subject institutions to certain standards, including political, religious, and philosophical criteria. Only schools cooperating with the party agenda will receive approval. This discrimination will begin in a subtle manner in 2013 and will accelerate in subsequent years of progressive rule. Many of the current institutions will go out of existence.

Religion

Religious expression will be severely limited in Obama Two. The usual holiday celebrations will be subject to restriction. At first it will be controlled allegedly because the public display of religious expression is of such a nature that it offends the sensibilities of nonbelievers. Eventually local energy regulating entities will object to public utilities accommodating explicitly religious displays.

In public intellectual life, religious expression will default to Jenkinsianism. This is a position developed by John Jenkins, president of the University of Notre Dame, which is essentially the promotion of the intellectual deficiency in religious teaching. Mr. Jenkins invited Obama to his university and helped advance the new president's message. Obama shortly thereafter expressed what is essentially Jenkinsianism. It maintains that there is a false dichotomy erected by religious leaders between religion and the progressive scientific agenda. This agenda includes making public support for abortion integral to women's health care, the use of embryonic stem cells, and any other progressive program that will develop. As we'll see in later chapters, the pragmatism underlying progressive activities provides a definition and limitation for religious faith.

Pragmatic holdings supported by Jenkinsianism

The problem with individual religious faiths such as Catholicism is that the proponents of the religion simply don't understand their own religion correctly. This deficiency is reflected in the ludicrous public statements to the effect that there is opposition between religious faith and the modern scientific-backed agenda of the administration. The invitation to Obama to speak at a Catholic University led support to this thesis.

No matter how long he continues to breathe, Jenkins will never be able to undo in the minds of countless youths this concept which is a crucial weapon in the progressive armament against all established religion: religious people are ignorant of their own religious holdings.

Since pragmatism defines acceptable religious dimensions, we can expect to see increasing limitations placed on freedom of religion and the eventual disappearance of genuine religious institutions as operating entities.

Free Speech

We have already detailed how free speech will be curtailed with media control. The enactment of EU laws effecting political correctness will occur by 2015.

Surveillance of citizens: publication of hate crimes

Cell phone recordings of violations of political correctness will be fed immediately to YouTube. At first segments of the population (e.g. minorities) will willingly feed recordings of fellow citizen violations. By 2018 the administration will have shed its veneer, and, as the more sinister characteristics of government programs become well-known, citizen-informing will drop off considerably.

Conclusion: the twelve steps of population impact

The following are the steps the population under progressive rule will take:

1. Hope—this occurred in the period before the 2012 election.
2. Disappointment—the result of the 2012 election of Obama.
3. Discouragement—the belief develops that a representative government is an impossibility.
4. Stress/rage—this will be in reaction to measures enacted by government they resent.
5. Fear—the realization that penalties, including fines and imprisonment, can result from noncompliance.
6. Devastation—the experience of substantial losses due to government fines and penalties.
7. Aimlessness—the purposeless existence that follows the above stages.
8. Divinement—the self-searching and openness to transcending hope.
9. Nesting—the turning to individual human relationships for personal support and encouragement.
10. Networking—the more organized addressing of problems and sharing of solutions within a group.
11. Equality—the achievement of results sufficient to sustain aspirations of change.
12. Supremacy—the defeat of government tyranny and/or measures destructive to human life.

CHAPTER 21

Militia

We cannot continue to rely only on our military in order to achieve the national security objectives that we've set. We have got to have a civilian national security force that's just as powerful, just as strong, just as well-funded.

The above statement by candidate Barack Obama in July of 2008 ignited a flurry of responses from conservatives, followed by immediate replies from liberals. To some right-leaning sources, the statement smacked of downright "here we go again"- We're back to Brown Shirts/Gestapoism. Quoting Representative Paul Broun, "That's exactly what Hitler did in Nazi Germany and it's exactly what the Soviet Union did."

The Annenberg Foundation replied, "This false claim is a badly distorted version of Obama's call for doubling the Peace Corps, creating volunteer networks and increasing the size of the Foreign Service." The Obama statement, Annenberg claimed, should be read in context with the rest of Obama's statement.

True enough. In Colorado Springs Obama promised, "As president I will expand AmeriCorps to 250,000 slots, double the size of the Peace Corps by 2011 to renew our diplomacy. People of all ages, stations and skills will be asked to serve."

Not all "Right Leaning Blogs and Websites" bought into the Brown shirts/Gestapo interpretation. Many simply criticized the plan as another example of administration overspending. However, in February of 2009, President Obama's administration canceled a prior Clinton-term directive on the subject known as the "expeditionary workforce" and replaced it with a provision with some striking changes. The Clinton directive specifically dealt with overseas use of civilians. The word "overseas" is found nowhere in the new directive, and new terms like "restoration of order" and "stability of operations" are featured prominently.

The Posse Comitatus Act of 1878 limited the powers of the federal government to use the military for law enforcement'; that is, to keep it from becoming the policeman on your block.. But in January 2009, Rep. Bob Filner quietly introduced a new bill, H.R. 675, that would amend title 10 of the United States Code and extend to civilian employees of the Department of Defense the authority to execute warrants, make arrests, and carry fire-arms. Some observers found this effort to bypass Posse Comitatus troubling and questioned whether we were looking at the beginning of the Obama national force.

Consideration

We have already noted that progressives, like their Hegelian counterpart, the antithesis, accept violence as an essential part of the agenda of change; to change requires violence; therefore, people in favor of change usually endorse the use of force.

Even if the Annenberg Foundation is correct in assessing Obama's plan to expand the Peace Corps, this does not exclude the creation of a potentially coercive force. The Peace Corps, for example, has been associated with compulsive sterilization agendas: the Quechuan Indian women abuse in Bolivia is a well-documented example of this. The involvement of altruistic youths in carrying out aggressive government programs is compatible with the history of younger age Americans being highly supportive of progressive programs.

Scenario for the creation of a militia

Our scenario forecasts the Obama administration's erection of a national social force of sizeable magnitude by mid-2016. What are the steps necessary to achieve this?

The first step is the integration of the US military as government workers. The heroic accomplishments of servicemen will have parity with civilian government workers' demonstration of progressive party loyalty and service in areas of womens health and the good job done in the identification of predjudicial acts by offending citizens. Military personnel who are reluctant to accept the equivalence of their service in armed conflict with civilian political agendas will be kept in check by the ever constant hint of investigation of possible abusive activity in past conflicts (e.g. middle east). Seductive financial awards comparable to income increases for government civilian administrators will also provide incentive.

Veterans' grievances, especially in regard to complaints with the health services received through the Veterans Administration, have been mostly neglected by society, but the Democratic Party and progressive organizations have been more responsive and will use this to achieve veteran support.

Professional military leaders will be unwilling to associate themselves with previous progressive-endorsed public demonstrations, particularly with the mob-dominated Wall Street occupiers. To accommodate the necessary professionalism of the military, the Obama administration will rid themselves of most of these protesters. This is another demonstration of how progressive regimes deal with once necessary but no longer useful elements. Other progressive regimes, such as Germany's Third Reich had to dispose of the Brown Shirts to get the cooperation of the German General Corps. At their wholesale execution, the confused early supporters proclaimed with their dying words "Heil Hitler." We can certainly expect the same for Obama supporters as he rids the country of the obstacle of distracting street protestors.

Once he has gained control of the military through an initial alliance with key military segments, Obama can now proceed with the long-term Communist goal of defanging capitalism. He has already taken a substantial step toward demoralizing the quality of soldiering when he achieved the "don't ask, don't tell" victory of civil rights. In the past most soldiers didn't really pay that much attention to the sexual orientation of their comrades. In the army, sex life really played no role for the average soldier. Gays have always served sometimes, even making excellent leaders without much ado about their sexuality. On leave, soldiers sought out whatever partner suited their sexual orientation.

With the new policy, sexuality will now be defined, and with it will come sexual privilege. One can be heterosexual in the military without indulging in heterosexual activity. The navy actually frowns on some aspects of heterosexuality, such as infidelity among officers. The new act sanctions not only the orientation but also the sexual practice itself.

Denigration of cultural ideology

What started out as the granting of civil rights to all to participate in military service will actually become an important force in the denigration of cultural inheritance. Chaplains will have difficulty advising those whose religious belief disallows homosexual acts.

There is another aspect of culture that will be at risk. Western military draws its culture from the Spartan model. This sets Western armies apart from all others. The Spartan communal combat rule "return with your shield or on it" was actually a maternal bidding. Women bred warriors in many ways. This feminine expectation gave birth to an integration of the military with the rest of society. The association of the military with homosexual activity breaks this societal bond.

A further erosion of culture will be achieved through denationalization goals. The US military will be increasingly integrated into NATO and other units not under American leadership.

Elimination of the military

If necessary, the military can also be controlled by another progressive tactic: encourage defection. This was used by the progressive Russian Socialists to undermine the Imperial Russian Army in World War I. Modern warfare offers a marvelously efficient technique—nuclear skirmishes that become more plausible with each passing day. Having once faced the devastation of the nuclear battlefield, many will show reluctance to engage this certain horror even when ordered to do so.

Defection, of course, has its risks. In the American tradition, defection bears the stigma of disgrace—another behavioral characteristic from the Spartan inheritance. Still there is the possibility that today's defector may become tomorrow's revolutionary. Pelosi wisely spoke of the need to be watchful of veterans. The Russian Revolution was aided by the deactivated veterans crowding the streets of Moscow. Adequate programs should keep them in check.

Another method to effect military extinction is outright abandonment. We have seen this before in history: Napoleon's army was a nuisance. His battle was not proceeding well, and it was slowing up his career advancement. Bonaparte abandoned thousands of French soldiers to die on the sands of Egypt as he himself returned to France as the man of the hour and was awarded a new army.

Finally, if you have the political strength, you can simply use lack of funding to whittle down the military. Obama has already proposed a much-reduced military budget. In good time Obama will accomplish the defanging of capitalism, the dream of every central-planning Communist seeking to spread world order.

Organization: creating the militia

We have talked about the ways the Obama administration can control or eliminate the current military structures, but how is it possible to put together an army? It's really not all that hard.

Actually progressives have given us an excellent example of doing just that in post-WWI Germany.

After the war, restrictions were placed on the number of active duty troops that defeated Germany could have. The army staff responded with the "placard virtual army." Each man represented not an individual soldier but rather a division of some kind. Soldiers carried a placard about the neck and were trained and communicated daily at the imagined command level as though they had several thousands of men. This allowed the few allotted troops to deal with disposition of equipment and perform problem solving exercises with representations of manpower units that didn't yet exist. When the time came, however they knew what to do with the influx of recruits.

In the same way, the Obama progressives can select both seasoned leaders and new leaders from the various Youth Corps Activities. Using the "Bottom- Up" approach, the administration can incorporate local organizations into the new militia structure.

Militia engagements

Despite putting together an adequate force, the progressive regime will see few conflicts. The force is designed for internal control, to keep potential opposition in check while the progressive changes proceed. Financial harassment will have already produced a much-cowed American nation; actual physical opposition will be too poorly organized and come too late to earn any sympathy from the public. Most incidents will be simply from frustration and will carry an irrational tone. The majority of the nation will side with the restoration of public order via the new national militia.

Southern border vulnerability

The southern US border with Mexico will continue the leave the United States vulnerable to increased drug trafficking. The one-world global government model will not be not sufficiently in place, but the Obama administration will allow the border to remain open despite some negative effects, including increased corruption of government officials. Efforts to shut down the border would be offensive not only to Americans of Hispanic ancestry but also to the internationalist movement that strives for borderless countries.

The single best example of free enterprise during the next 2000 days will actually be the illegal drug trade involving US-Mexico border activity. Later chapters will reveal how a greatly enhanced drug trade, even if drugs are legalized, will be the surprisingly fatal challenge to the tyranny of progressive rule.

CHAPTER 22

The Arc at Zenith

**Introduction-Andy Stern Discusses a five year plan-
Conclusion: abandon the election process.**

In November 2011 Andy Stern, president of the Service Employees
International Union (SEIU), traveled to China as part of a dialog between a US contingent and high-ranking Chinese government officials. The controversial trip was organized by the Center
for American Progress and the China-US Exchange Foundation.
Stern found the Communist regime's agenda extremely attractive;
it underscored much of the progressive goals: $640 billion invest-
ment in renewable energy, clean engine vehicles, and better environmental protection. But then he notes an important feature of
the plan was that it covered a five-year period, typical of centrally
planned economies such as China and the former Soviet Union.

   Stern: "Some Americans are drawing lessons from this."

   These Americans would include Orville Schell, Asian Society
director of the Center on US-Chinese Relations, who stated, "I
think we have come to realize the ability to plan is exactly what is
missing in America." Also in agreement is Robert Engle, who won
a Nobel Prize in 2003 for economics, who states "while China is

making five-year plans for the next generation, Americans are planning only for the next election."

An important question

Considering the relationship of the progressive agenda and the attraction of a five-year plan as the most suitable method for achieving desirable objectives, might there develop a mandate to end the election process as we know it? Now, it's a rather serious leap to suggest that the Obama administration would eliminate the election process, but the trend as of 2013 will be toward consolidation of power.

Wouldn't that mean a dictatorship? A dictatorship in America? Well, yes, but does that really seem incredible, considering we have already witnessed expressions of dictatorial overtones? In the case of Fox News, we have seen White House attempts to eliminate criticism; "We call them as we see them." Obama stated on a TV interview, immune to the illogic of his statement since he acted against a broadcast organization that merely called *him* like they see him.

In a State of the Union address, with the black-robed justices of the Supreme Court sitting not far away, President Obama took aim at a recent court decision that said corporations could spend as much as they wanted to sway voters in federal elections. "Last week, the Supreme Court reversed a century of law to open the floodgates for special interests—including foreign companies-to spend without limit in our elections," Obama declared. "Well, I don't think American elections should be bankrolled by America's most powerful interests, and worse, by foreign entities. They should be decided by the American people, and that's why I'm urging Democrats and Republicans to pass a bill that helps to right this wrong."

Analysis

Supreme Court ruling is the law of the land, the final arbiter on an issue presented to us as a nation. It can, of course, be overturned by subsequent cases, especially when something new or different occurs and social change requires it. But until then it has always been considered the law of the land.

Complaint of elections being bankrolled by America's most powerful interests is a joke—Obama's election was bankrolled by probably the world's richest and most powerful man. His biggest contributor was the unions, including SEIU. The statement about foreign entities was simply untruthful. Again Obama utilizes the Alinsky protocol of telling lies to achieve goals.

Obama's statement about countermanding the court through legislation doesn't make sense at first blush. Even if the legislature wrote a bill on an issue that the court has ruled against, it would most likely not be law. But Obama's real purpose should be understood: it was to get the public thinking about pitting legislation and the American people against the court.

Compare Obama's lack of leadership with the way previous presidents handled unpopular decisions. Kennedy got the "No more prayer at school" decision. Kennedy's response: Let's pray more at home. Eisenhower got the integration support order. To a fifties crowd he taught: we don't pick and choose which of our laws we'll follow. The Obama administration inherited that system of government that prevailed, the system where one branch of government acknowledges the other.

Chief Justice Roberts, who has gone to every annual presidential address to Congress since taking his seat in 2005, suggested in March that he had misgivings about continuing that practice. Bloomberg notes the following:

"The image of having the members of one branch of government standing up, literally surrounding the Supreme Court, cheering and hollering while the court, according to the requirements of protocol, has to sit there expressionless, I think is very troubling," Roberts told law students at the University of Alabama. "And it does cause you to think whether or not it makes sense for us to be there."

Alito expressed similar misgivings in October. He said the event had become awkward for the justices, forcing them to sit "like the proverbial potted plant."

Exploitation of the judiciary

It's important to note the courts, including the United States Supreme Court, have limited power of enforcement. They rely on the executive branches to carry that out. Obama, however, has committed his administration to selective enforcement, reserving for himself unlawful powers. He openly declared the Defense of Marriage Act unconstitutional and instructed the attorney general not to enforce it. Only one political figure, then presidential candidate Herman Cain, spoke out about this, declaring it an impeachable offense.

The Obama takeover plan has already targeted the legislature. When Paul Ryan made a budget proposal, Obama first praised him then invited him to be present in a session while he attacked him. Obama made blatant attempts to curtail powers of the legislature through passage of the Health Care Act, which calls for extensive appointments of key individuals, bypassing the customary legislative confirmation. Add to this his statement that he would do everything he could without legislature and you can easily conclude that Obama has introduced something foreign to the office of the President of the United States.

Check on democratization

Consider the following checks on the Democratic process that now exist:

- Obama supported the elimination of secret ballots in labor union elections.

- Democratic caucuses do not use secret ballots in nominations.

Consider also statements of progressives to the effect that we would be better off with less democracy. North Carolina

Democratic Governor Beverly Perdue recommends suspending congressional elections for the next couple of years as a way to solve the national debt crisis. Matthew Boye presented her statements on the *Daily Caller* website: "Perdue said she thinks that temporarily halting elections would allow members of Congress to focus on the economy. 'You have to have more ability from Congress, I think, to work together and to get over the partisan bickering and focus on fixing things,' Perdue said."

A spokesman said later that Perdue was only joking, but the notion is certainly in line with progressive motivations. Peter Orszag introduced a similar argument in a *New Republic* article stating, "We need less democracy." Here again supporters were quick to argue that he was misunderstood, that "Orszag is really worried about the way party polarization leads to paralyzing gridlock in our system." Of course, if it was the agenda of the Republican Party that was suffering from gridlock due to Democratic ability to filibuster, we may easily assume Orszag would be silent.

Forecast: Demise of the Electoral College

The US government will lose its representative system of government before the end of Obama's second term. Growing Alinsky-style agitation against the Electoral College, along with the increasing acceptance of the Constitution as a living document without absolute guarantees, will eliminate the election process.

As a popular measure, a nationwide referendum will be held in lieu of elections in 2016. Many will consent to this as a last-ditch effort to stave off the complete loss of a democratic republic. They will be completely mistaken. Obama's team will once again triumph as the nation gets caught up in the notion of "finally being able to get things done." Important factors in promoting the referendum will be an urgency to enforce a green agenda and the election of the president by popular vote. This will be supported by an extensive media campaign.

Obstacles to the referendum of 2016 will be delineated and eliminated

Even if there is a majority who disagree with the referendum, they will very likely be silent, cowed by fear of social militia enforcement. Institutional opposition will be scant; what little remains of religious expression will be controlled or ridiculed.

The Control of Institutional Religion as an Obstacle to the Progressive Agenda:

How the Catholic Church will disappear from public life: The Goodmanic Formulation and The New Atheism.
On November 6, 2011, a Sunday morning issue of the *Chicago Sun-Times* carries the image of a rather attractive blonde girl beside the headline, "How Dare You?" Her conversation in bold print was directed to Cardinal George of the Chicago Archdiocese: "How dare you tell me what choice to make when I didn't have a choice when I was raped."

What were the facts behind this dramatic front page? The abortion rights group Personal PAC scheduled an award ceremony for Goodman for her work as counselor at a rape crisis center. The Catholic Governor Pat Quinn was to make an appearance to make the award. The cardinal condemned the governor for going "beyond a political alignment with those supporting the legal right to kill children in their mother's womb to rewarding those deemed most successful in this terrible work."

It turns out that Goodman, also a rape victim, stated she never personally referred a woman for an abortion, and, although she admits supporting politicians that advanced that option, she took offense to being called "a baby killer."

It could be easily argued that Quinn represents a certain trendy group termed *Real Katoliques*. While proclaiming themselves practicing Catholics, they largely reject the notion of perennial wisdom in favor of a form of pragmatism. The *Real Katolique* pragmatism regards the Catholic Church as an institution saddled with anachronistic tendencies. Like pragmatists, they place great faith in the concept of time yielding truth. The contemporary Catholic Church with its trappings of papacy and absolute doctrines, all so incompatible with their personal beliefs, are merely temporal artifacts certain to dissipate with time. They point to past incidents of church disputes with Galileo and Copernicus as evidence of this.

A closer study of the Goodman-George issue reveals the features of social interactions that in Obama Two will lead to the extinguishment of religious expression in public life. Breaking down the conflict into key elements will reveal a formula; there is:

1. **Church responsibility of religious belief**— In Goodman, a religious leader becomes concerned about the scandal of a public figure touting himself as being Catholic but supporting abortion activities.

2. **Public action or expression**—the religious leader openly condemns the public figure.

3. **The collateral effect**- A young rape victim is distressed.

4. **The Alinsky attack truth**- Women who are rape victims are reluctant to seek help and are in need of compassion).

5. **Liability**—the damage that accrues to church or faithful)-The religious leader is blasted in the press as lacking compassion.

6. **Response of Church or faithful**— A reluctance to speak out about public figures.

We can apply this formula to health care, education, and other issues that will develop in Obama Two.

Goodmanic Formulation:

Issue	Obligation from faith.	Public action	Collateral effect	The Alinsky attack truth	Church Liability	Church Response.
Goodman	Avoid public Scandal	Condemn Public Leader	Distress of Young Rape Victim	Rape victims need compassion	Blasted in Press as lacking compassion.	Reluctance to speak out about Catholic Public Figures.
Health Care	individual conscience in matters of abortion & contraception	Refusal to participate in abortion or issuance of contraceptives.	Woman's right to health care is affected.	Childbirth endangers the life and health of the mother.	Civil and/or criminal law suits.	Withdrawal from working in the area of health care.
Freedom of Sex Act.	Teaching faithfully on matters of sexuality	Teaching extra-marital sex and homosexual acts are wrong.	church teaching offends societal groups.	morality give rise to contempt for homosexuality	Civil and/or criminal lawsuits.	Teaching on sexuality and performing marriages, according to religious faith will be done in secret.
Human Rights.	Teaching on subsidiarity and human freedoms.	Challenge governments actions on parental controls.	impedes progressive agenda	religion interferes with advancing social projects.	Civil and/or criminal lawsuits for sedition and hate speech. .	Avoid public statements and actions.

The new atheism

The second important control mechanism to prevent opposition to the progressive agenda is the new atheism—a movement
of best-selling atheist writers who advocate that "religion should
not simply be tolerated, but should be countered, criticized, and
exposed by rational arguments wherever its influence arises."
The advancement of science mandates the elimination of religion. The progressive movement during Obama's second term
will further this view, which will have a significant impact, particularly on younger voters.

Conclusion

The next presidential election is scheduled to occur in November
2016. It will not occur, or if it does, it will in a highly diminished
form with only token resistance to the progressive supremacy.

PART FIVE

The Thoroughly Negotiated Moral

CHAPTER 23

Pragmatism
and Religion

By the beginning of 2016, the American people will have lost two major freedoms that are considered essential to a free society: the freedom of speech and freedom of religious expression. The previous chapters showed the forces that would create this unprecedented transformation in American life.

To succeed, however, the progressive ascendency requires an additional leveling of institutions and philosophies that have been the safeguards of individual freedoms since the establishment of the republic. The next four chapters will reveal how these safeguards were eroded beginning with the adoption of "Pragmatism," a philosophy that developed into the "Social Acid" that eroded liberty.

What exactly is Pragmatism ? Well, if you want exactly, it is difficult to define. So many variations have developed over the years. We can probably best think of it as essentially limiting our knowledge and other things to experience. The source of all theories and the validity of knowledge is based on experience. For example, suppose you noticed that you are more productive at work when you rest up at the end of the weekend. You then conclude that the answer to how you can be more productive at work is by resting on weekends. Notice that you didn't start out by first asking the question, "What should I do to be more productive during the week?" You made an observation from experience, and that gave rise to the question. This is sort of how pragmatism operates. It is sometimes called radical empiricism. One can see how it can work out as a self-help device. Your experience leads to knowledge about yourself and how to improve. The problem develops when we attempt to put all knowledge and theory on this experiential model.

Where did pragmatism come from?

The philosophy of pragmatism began to develop at the end of the nineteenth century. It was an exciting time of scientific discoveries and intellectual ferment accompanied by a surge in man's confidence to put the study of human psychology on a scientific level. This newfound confidence came from the study of physical phenomena. The work of Helmholtz provided an important clue.

Consider what happens when you are looking at a billiard table. A ball is sitting motionless in the center of the table. Someone strikes another ball, gets it rolling. It collides with the ball in the center and, almost magically, the moving ball comes to a stop and the motionless ball begins to move.

From the study of such phenomena came important concepts of energy. Energy goes from one ball to the other. In the late nineteenth century, people realized that the same energy that moved the billiard ball could be converted into an electric current or into light and back to energy of movement. This transformation of energy that hides at one moment and reveals itself in the next was a powerful model for understanding human behavior. The integral relation of the energy transformation and the particular event during which it occurred was especially intriguing for some philosophers.

Darwinism enters the bedroom

The late nineteenth century was also a time of Darwin's influence. The theory of evolution played an important role in the development of pragmatism. With the revelation of man as a derivative of animal life, scientists became less respectful of the traditional boundaries of the human body. Bilroth surgically invaded the peritoneum to do unprecedented operations on the bowel, and Freud pried into the most personal human thoughts, revealing intimate sexual experiences of the upper levels of society. Into this milieu came William James—philosopher, psychologist, and one of the most important names in the development of pragmatism.

Is religion unscientific?

James had a background in both science and religious faith. He had a degree in medicine from Harvard; his father was an eccentric Wedenborgen theologian. James wanted to give religion some validity, and he rejected those who said, from a logical scientific viewpoint, that religious faith was merely delusional. His approach was to look at evolution and say that it tells us that man has come about by surviving years of precarious events. Here we are today, and the fact that we survived has value. In the same sense, if we look at someone going through life who has a religious belief, we might notice that this religious belief plays an important role in the person having confidence, getting things done in life. Therefore, James would argue that religion has value, that it is defined as a truth by experience.

Things to note here:

There is no vindication of things per se in religion. There is no absolute truth since truth is defined by experience alone. And other dimensions of religion, such as established liturgy and doctrines would be considered overreligious and not legitimate according to experience.

Progressivism will acknowledge religion, but only as defined by pragmatism. Putting this another way, progressives will define your faith for you. That is why Obama maintains that there is no dichotomy between religious faith and his "science" and why feminists will stress that there is no issue of religious freedom in the matter of contraceptive coverage by religious organizations. They have decided what can and cannot be religious faith.

The real danger of pragmatism

This now gets us to the real threat of pragmatism. The philosophy leads to the changing, continuous development of ideas, such as human individuality and liberty. This is why some call it the "social acid" that dissolves liberty.

By understanding this philosophy, we can now see why Al Gore refers to the Constitution as a "living, breathing document." The liberties declared therein are subject to negotiation.

First come the social reforms, the Alinsky Agenda, the Jaffe Memorandum. Then you define liberty within that framework. Some authors, such as Kloppenberg, have commented on Obama's intellectual background, such as it is, making note of pragmatism in the formation of his ideas. The problem with Kloppenberg's statement is that he neglected the Alinsky component to Obama. Using the Alinsky perspective one can never be certain that Obama tells the truth. I refer to this as the "Kloppenberg incompleteness." It is essentially a poorly done analysis of Obama's concept of Pragmatism.

Erection of social reforms so integral to pragmatic politics involves organization, which therefore requires the development of bureaucratic power. Thus, we see the emergence the American *apparatchik* and Durbanism. The new society is to be based on planning. The consensus of the popular will, in the end, is not necessary.

CHAPTER 24

The non-Adlerian State

Wolfboys really do exist

Doctors expressed shock at finding a boy (possibly ten years old) living with a pack of wolves in a remote forest in the Kaluga region of central Russia. It was noted that this was not unprecedented. Apparently, in economic hard times in Russia a number of abandoned children have been raised by animals.

What was the child like?

He snarled, couldn't speak, walked on all long-nailed fours. How did he get like that? If we suppose that we have descended from animals, maybe something beastly remains in us. But the boy's DNA didn't change all that much from when he was born. Is he really human now? And some religious believers might ask, "Does he have a soul?"

Consider how man comes to know that he is a man vs. a cow or a dog. Philosophers have long believed that our knowledge of things begins in sense experience. The physical informs the mind, and, in theological terms, the body informs the soul. That is the only way we can know. We know something because we experience it. But the knowledge that I am a man comes from the experience of longstanding observance of other men, seeing in them the meaning of what it means to be human.

To know who and what we are requires society

What happens, however, when we become aware that the society that gave us our identity turns out to be distinctly human? When we find out it falters? When we become aware of the defects of the collective action of the society? We learn that our society bombs innocent families and children, that this society enforces slavery and segregation. There is then a tendency to disown the source of your identity, to hold the society unworthy in a mode similar to parent-child disownership.

That disposition toward society is prevalent today and is especially represented in the progressive outlook. One asks how is it that Bill Ayers, who bombed buildings in the '60s, or Jane Fonda who aided enemies of the United States during the Vietnam War are able to thrive in the States. A university accepted Ayers as a professor; Fonda sustained a film career. How is it that there is no liability as a result of their actions?

The answer is that, in the modern collective mind-set, the United States is simply unworthy of respect. Because of things past, we have developed a mass acceptance of unworthiness. Disrespect for the flag is quite okay; take a crap on it if you like.

Neither Ayres nor Fonda have ever expressed the slightest apology for their actions. Ayers said he wished he had bombed more. What others perceive as a country, a society, the progressive mind-set sees as nothing more than a mass, transformable without constraints. There's no problem with open borders. What right has the government to stop people? Nothing in law is absolute; there is nothing we can't and shouldn't change if we feel like it. No reason why we should be more concerned with the country we live in than with other countries of the world. Our country is merely an address.

What Obama leaves out

Alinsky in his *Rules for Radicals* stated that the United States should apologize for Vietnam. Following his mentor, Obama has been observed doing just this, apologizing while visiting with foreign dignitaries. But what is lacking from Alinsky is the other half of the deal. It is this: Yes we have sinned, but we, with all our faults and accepting our shame, are a nation that strives for perfection, to be a nation with superior virtues and values. We humbly seek a chance to try again, for the chance to have our actions speak for these high qualities.

To add the Alinsky deficit, to his failure to include the quest for perfection requires something completely lacking in the progressive agenda— love. From the Christian perspective, this love is not some declaration of an intense nationalism; rather it is always an appreciation for the fundamental gift of society that has informed you as to who you are, the collective loving of your neighbor. Fonda /Ayers radicals have no love for the country that has fallen. There is no saying, "What a terrible thing that has happened; how can we make it better? What can we do for this society, this mass of fellowship that I love?" Obama routinely distances himself from his countrymen with an attitude of "They did those things, not me." Simply put, to care requires a sharing of shame. When George Washington said, "My country, right or wrong," he was not being arrogant. "If it's wrong, with God's help, let me make it right" is what he implied—a sharing of shame, saying this is me and my beloved.

Progressives don't have a love for a country but rather for what can be transformed out of itself. It is only the new, the not yet existing, that can be loved.

Adler vs. Freud

Borrowing from psychology, we can apply two different kinds of developmental models in understanding the above, namely that based on Freud and, by contrast, that of Adler. Again I'm going to oversimplify the positions of profound philosophers.

In studying problems with Freud, we start with a belief in a formative power at work in the deep, past, infantile neuroticism of human life. In society today it is Freudian theory that dominates. We look at racism as part of a deep-rooted pathological state. If someone objects to the current administration, it is chalked up to racism. Certain crimes are hate crimes because of something bad deep inside man.

What's really at stake here again is really shame avoidance. "Matthewism" is an excellent example of this. Consider the comments that Kevin Matthews consistently makes about Obama's opponents; this is highly suggestive of the fact that he is overcompensating for the insecurity he himself experiences about his own feelings of racism. He sees racism in the thoughts of every white man not in agreement with Obama. This is a typical Freudian analysis.

In contrast with Freud's theory we have that of Adler. The two men were in disagreement about very basic issues. Adler's psychology has been described as teleological; that is, oriented toward goals, whereas Freud focused on dynamics of the make up of the human psyche. Adler describes the mature and positive person as someone with a high social interest. This person is concerned about family and friends and society in general. Adler uses the concept of social interest as a very important indicator of psychological health. This relationship between the individual well-being and that of society is what is missing in the radical personality. Recall the value of society in telling us who we are; the wolfboy doesn't know he is man because society was absent in his life.

From inferiority to superiority

In Adler's goal-directed theory, there is a very natural process of development from inferiority to superiority. Perhaps the first social relationship in this developmental pathway is that between infant and mother. Adler considers this relationship as an example of the nature of social interest. Both mother and infant are in need of love, and out of that need the infant satisfies his hunger as he relieves the mother's milk-filled breast; in such a way social interest may originate. Contrast Adler's concept of the mother-child relationship with that of Freud, who described the relationship of infant and mother as based in part on oral cannibalistic drives.

The two approaches may be summarized as follows:

Freud	Adler
neurosis from deep	natural process from
psychological processes	inferiority to superiority
difficult to treat	correctable by getting
years of therapy	back on natural process
country—no meaning	country—social interest
fellow citizens deeply disturbed	equals health.
relationships derive from	relationships derive from
evolutionary drives	love, leading to social interest

We said that the progressive ascendency requires neutralization of certain aspects of modern life. The undermining of love of country and the rejection of it as a worthy entity are part of the deal.

CHAPTER 25

The Sublimation of Husbandry

Introduction-

In his book *The Dubliners,* James Joyce recounts the story of a certain Mr. Doran, It was a situation not all that unfamiliar for those times. A single man going into middle age desires to find a young woman with all the attractive characteristics he dreams about. His plight typifies all the societal constraints on sexual desire and marriage on a young Catholic male. Marriage to such a woman entails the financial wherewithal not within Doran's grasp— and who knows when, or if, he can ever achieve it? So he succumbs to illicit sex with a madam's daughter and is trapped into a marriage with her.

Why do I mention this story in a book about a political scenario? It is because it has features to consider that impact our society as it heads into a prolonged period of progressive rule. These features include the constraints on fulfillment of human sexuality in a religious context and the economic resources and societal conventions that influence marriage.

The Catholic Church and sexuality

When I speak about religion, I frequently refer to the Catholic Church because I am more familiar with it than most other faiths and also because it represents a major component of Western Cultural Heritage. At the time of Vatican II in the 1960s, many felt that the Church would make a change in its teaching on human sexuality. There had been big break-throughs in regulating pregnancy using "the pill." The new guy they elected pope was of the liberal bent and into a lot of modern philosophers. Surely this Paul VI would update Catholic teaching on sex.

Instead he declared contraceptive use illicit. The explosive controversy that followed his encyclical "Humanae Vitae" is now historical. How could he fail to address the erotic aspects of human existence even as he himself was the recipient of charges that he actually indulged in them?

There are really two issues here. First, the reasons he affirmed traditional teaching and second, the response of the bishops, pastors, and theologians throughout the world.

In America the reaction was similar to the response to the shame of slavery—a sublimation. Clerical resistance to "Humanae Vitae" was rampant. This time, the movement involved conscience as the criteria for sexual life. The reasoning went like this: It's up to couples to decide what to do about having children and their fertility. The church always taught it's sinful to go against what your conscience tells you. My conscience tell me it's A-OK to use oral contraceptives. Therefore I can use them and be consistent with Catholic belief."

But for Catholics there was an alternative to "The Pill" !

But there was a science of husbandry available in the '60s that was just as effective as the pill but was not opposed to Church teaching. This was the Billings Ovulation Method developed by John Billings and confirmed by scientists James Brown, who performed the first in-vitro fertilization in England, and Eric Oldeblad from Sweden.

Even today the method has been greatly misrepresented and confused with an early, ineffective attempt at birth control used by the Catholic Church called "the rhythm method." To their discredit, some obstetrics and gynecology and biology texts are still unable to correctly discuss Billings or, what is just as incompetent, the authors confuse it with the now-defunct rhythm method.

The Billings is an all-natural, easy-to-learn-and-use program with a 99 percent effective rate confirmed in large-scale studies in both China and India. More than 50 million couples worldwide are involved in the use of the Billings method. Studies also confirm a far lower divorce rate trend in Billing users compared with users of other birth control methods.

You would think that, given such valuable information on reproduction management acceptable to Church teachings, this would be something that the Church would actively install and every parish. However, it appears that there is considerable resistance. Most parishes give only token support to promoting natural family planning, and when Billings practitioners seek to develop a program in the parish, the group is often informed that the parish does not wish any "outsiders" promoting natural family planning.

What is really behind this resistance? The most logical explanation is that pastors really don't want to threaten the conscience of their congregation. A method such as Billings would question the practice common among many Catholics—the acceptance of oral contraceptives by way of a negotiated conscience.

Thesis: Catholic Parishes Don't Firmly Support Natural Family Programs Out of Fear of Losing Contributions From Conscience-Mediated Parishioners on Contraceptives.

This is an example of "reverse Axelrodianism." The Lenin Corollary of Axelrodianism states that criticism creates a new agenda and must be eliminated. Here a new agenda implies criticism. There is a good chance that promotion of natural family planning in parishes could offend some Catholics and there of course might be financial consequences for the parish bank accounts. The promotion of the Billings Method in the face of widespread accommodation to oral contraceptives on the basis of conscience is therefore something parishes would prefer to avoid at all costs.

Sublimation agenda for husbandry

As with the avoidance of shame, desertion of truth in the matter of husbandry manifests itself with a sublimation agenda. Pick up any bulletin from a Catholic church and you won't find a parish office to assist with husbandry such as onsite teaching of Billings. But you will find an office of ministry of peace and justice, something parish members feel far more comfortable with. Again it is the ubiquitous agenda of peace and justice that buries the gift of knowledge of parenting, and society pays an enormous price for this deficit.

And what are the fruits of this sublimated agenda? The Church will frequently point to the families and elderly helped by programs like the Campaign for Human Development, but the truth is that every year enormous Church funds, which are mostly left in the hands of a progressive team, will underwrite activities not in conformance with Catholic doctrines. This is not surprising: Alinsky, in his writings, earmarked rudderless churches and morally confused groups such as the Jesuits as easily acquired vehicles for accomplishing his goals. When this work is exposed for what it is, the sponsoring bishops reply that anyone who criticizes merely hates the Church. It is interesting to note the similarity between the bishops' response and that of Matthewism. Anyone critical of Obama has deep-seated thoughts of racism; anyone criticizing the Alinsky agenda has a pathological hatred of the Church. Freudian psychology trumps Adlerian. But the fact still remains: The divorce rate among Catholics in the Alinsky program using artificial contraception is far higher than among those that practice natural family planning. The higher divorce rate is easily found among the fruits of modern parish agendas.

The Church minimizes its neglect of husbandry probably because, according to many Church documents, it anticipates that the Hispanic immigration, the future of the American parishes, will be more than sufficient to provide a parishioner base. That arrogance may be short-lived as Hispanics are increasingly finding other religions more compatible with family life. It is an interesting fact that most Mormons today are Spanish-speaking. Perhaps it is because Mormons are actively pro-life.

Sexuality affects society

Adler supports the idea that the most fundamental act of justice is the human sexual act. If that is so, how can one speak of justice while ignoring the foundation of all acts of justice and not expect it to have an effect on society? In fact, progressives are well aware of the power of sex when it comes to impacting society.

For example, consider what happened under Stalin's program, which required the seizure of land from the Russian peasants but encountered resistance from traditional Russian families. To undermine family structure, and therefore family control of farmlands, Stalin advanced the "glass of water" theory of sex. They would promote to farmwives the notion that having sex is just like having a glass of water; both acts merely quench a thirst. Therefore men and women should not let marriage prevent them from the enjoyment of such a basic thing.

But, as one spiritual writer observes, sex refuses to reduce itself. Look at how many murders, suicides, and assaults stem from sexual relations. The realization of the power of human sexuality can bring about radical changes of a different kind, changes that can benefit society.

This gets us back to Joyce's Mr. Dorran. Why is it so difficult for him to find love? Perhaps it's because of the way society is constructed, the notion that sex among the young should be neutralized or that it should be something they should abstain from like Mr. Dorran, until they have more resources. But why?

Skinner and canon law

Oddly enough it is behaviorist B.F Skinner that makes the case for a younger age for marriage. In *Walden Two* he gives these words to a character called Frazer:

> No doubt the thought of a girl getting married a year or two after she is ready for childbearing strikes you as something characteristic of primitive cultures or, worse still, backward communities in our own country.
>
> Certainly most girls are ready for childbearing at fifteen or sixteen. We like to ridicule "puppy love." We say it won't last and judge its depth accordingly.
>
> Well, of course it doesn't last! A thousand forces conspire against it. And they are not the forces of nature, either, but of a badly organized society. The boy and girl are ready for love. They will never have the same capacity for love again. They're ready for marriage and childbearing. It's all part of the same thing. But society never lets them prove it.

Simply put, society is against early marriage because it goes against the flow. It requires a "free lunch." The younger couple is simply more likely to be needy and the rest of society doesn't like the idea they may have to help out.

But look at the religious point of view. Consider what the canon law says about marriage. The valid age according to Church law is fourteen years for the girl and sixteen for the boy. So the religion does not forbid early marriage. Where is the problem? Political? Economic?

New Perspective for Man: A younger age for marriage

Is it possible that the same forces that conspire against early marriage are the same that conspire against our enjoyment of sex?

Bill O'Reilly in his best seller *The O'Reilly Factor* suggests that our middle class existence leaves almost no time for sex. "Most of us work too hard to have much energy left over at the end of the day for serious romance, and the alarm goes off too early in the morning for a sunrise surprise."

But what if we change our economic planning around the objective of having more sex and having it in the relationship of marriage at an early age, even if society has to help out financially? Notice this is something both the left and right reject. For the left the idea violates the population-control imperative: everyone should support and encourage free contraceptives and abortion; no one should support free childbirth. For the right it's, "Don't have kids if you can't support them; that's not our problem."

But look at what happened in the period following World War II. The country engaged in fertility at an unprecedented rate, and the boom in babies was accompanied by a boom in the economy—something no one predicted. In France, the first signs of a recent improvement in the economy came with an increase in fertility of French women. In contrast the United States is barely at the population replacement rate and has experienced a sluggish economy.

National security depends on more sex?

No society can ever survive for any length of time that adopts as a priority the goal of making unrestricted access to contraception and abortion available for all women. It never has, nor ever will survive for long. Why is that?

The first and most obvious reason is that it leads to a decrease in life, but what is equally disastrous for society is that it leads to an increase in the conditionality of human life; existence of individual life is justified by social circumstances. This erects a slippery slope for elimination of the socially unpopular and, with that, society itself.

Second, there is an unwritten law in nature that says, "If you don't do it, someone else will." Look at the case of Italy. Italy is experiencing a population implosion sometimes called a "birth dearth." The fastest-growing population in Italy is not that of Italians. The country's negative replacement rates are so low that if they continue at this rate, within another 150 years there will be no more Italians. The Italian population is being replaced by a growing Muslim population. Author Peter Kreeft states that it is no wonder that the two most rapid growing religions are Mormons and Muslims: they are pro-life. Contrast the Muslim precepts: life is good, sex is oh so sweet, family is wonderful, Allah is great, with that of the Catholic Church's offering: neurotic avoidance of racial and/or gender prejudice, conscience-mediated self-sterilization.

The third reason is that the abortion mandate is incompatible with human existence. It empowers the negative; it is in opposition to the development of culture—of music, literature, and art of all forms. No culture that has espoused the reproduction-prevention agenda has ever been productive. Conception breeds innovation and creativity; contra-ception, with its emphasis on the negative, opposes it. Just look at the lack of cultural development in China compared with its financial growth and technological prowess.

Fourth, a lack of respect for women accompanies the cultural decline. The concept of the relationship between mother and child vanishes. It replaces the traditional image of women with a new species defined by the imitation of maleness—the "man-lette." This brings about a further decrease in fertility.

Conclusion

In our scenario, the failure of traditional sources in promoting the joy and value of creating new human life serves as a prelude to progressive liabilities including the loss of liberty and freedom of religious expression.

CHAPTER 26

White Supremacy and the Error of Civil Rights

In his 1978 Harvard commencement address, Aleksandr Solzhenitsyn stunned his audience. Western civilization, Solzhenitsyn offered, took a wrong turn at the time of the Renaissance when it sacrificed itself as a tradition of being God-centered, trading in spirituality for the historic progress of man. From that point on, the Nobel laureate, who had been the darling of the humanities establishment, quickly fell from grace as a result of his un-embracing statement of the progressive perspective. In a commemorative issue reviewing the last millennium, the *New York Times* didn't even give Solzhenitsyn the status of a Tim Russet or ex-CIA author Philip Agee.

In our contemporary mind-set, we hail the Renaissance as the beginning of true enlightenment. We could no more disparage the Renaissance than we could embrace a caveman existence. Without the development of the secular humanities, we would be lacking in democratic institutions, in civil rights, and in the advancement of science.

But we have already seen that some progressives have now taken a critical look at democracy as a hindrance to progress. At this point we turn to another possible source of opposition to democracy: that of the cultural conservative.

Perhaps no one in recent times has been more associated with the term "cultural conservative" than author and commentator William Buckley. Buckley gained fame for his critique of his alma mater, Yale University, in which he documented how the Ivy League institution "strayed from its original educational mission."

Buckley's opinions, regarded as "reckless generosity" by some, did a decent job of stirring things up, but as the era of civil rights began to flourish in the 1960s, the response to his views picked up a lot more heat. In an editorial in the *National Review* entitled "Why the South Must Prevail," Buckley spoke out explicitly in favor of white supremacy in the South.

Now some things should be kept in mind when reviewing Buckley's statement. First, Buckley was putting forth opinions based on rational arguments. While he was against civil rights legislation initially, he in no way sided with violent acts against the passage of the legislation. His argument was not that blacks were racially inferior, a point he never espoused, but rather that they were at that current time inferior with regard to a cultural and educational level compared with whites.

What does the second A stand for in NAACP?

Buckley adapted the literal meaning of the word "advancement" as found and its usage in the name NAACP. Advancement implied having been left behind. The goal was to achieve "genuine cultural equivalence among the races." How does one go about achieving this? Buckley felt that white people should remain in control while transferring cultural equality to black people. Buckley would surely stress education as well as stability in family life as key features in the process.

By the 1960s Buckley had changed his view. Violence was increasingly associated with the term "white supremacy." He opposed views of racial inferiority advanced by George Wallace (who eventually repented for his racism). Buckley then supported civil rights legislation.

Conservative opposition to democracy

What are some of the more general features of the conservative opposition to democracy? The leveling tendency in democracy not only leads to the opposite of superior culture transfer but also undermines the quest for human excellence. "Democracy jettisons heroic virtues and spiritual perfection. The quest for the philosophical truth becomes replaced by democratic tyranny."

The civil rights legislation corrected some blatant infringements on human liberties, but it failed to provide for family support. No measures were taken to develop equality of family structure between white families and black families. In fact, the welfare system that developed eroded the black family by requiring the absence of the husband in the house before payment could be received.

In addition, the civil rights legislation did nothing for the nation, which had failed in basic justice. There was no Adlerian correction. No embracement of shame and commitment to excellence. Instead it resulted in America as a country with violations of black civil liberties at every turn instead of an America that has completely reformed. Legislation divided the country into two groups: those that offend and those that are offended. Consider how Eric Holder, in dealing with violations of the basic right to vote, excused it by reference to past prejudice in American history. Notice there is no dividing line from America without racial justice to a nation of care. You can't have it both ways. Either you accept that the nation is worthy of support and love because it strives to right past wrongs or you admit that it is no longer a nation of laws and it's every man for himself (in which case the basic right to vote is unprotected).

Understandably there was a great deal of suspicion regarding Buckley's plan for genuine equality of culture between the races. But in the end, decades after the civil rights legislation, the current US statistics document persistent inequalities between blacks and whites. Blacks have a higher rate of crime and imprisonment, teenage pregnancy, and single-parent households; they also have lower educational achievements than their white counterparts. An argument can be made that this result is really the objective of progressive rule—maintain this disparity, and thereby maintain manipulation of social agendas. But such inequality does not reflect the goal of cultural conservatives.

PART SIX

The World
Order

CHAPTER 27

The Quest for
World Order

Here in our 2000-day scenario we make a major shift in focus. We go from the nationwide influences on the daily lives of Americans to global happenings. As stated earlier, to put together a reasonable forecast of the future for the United States means you need to also focus on what's going on in the rest of the world. As it turns out there is a very significant relationship between US and Global movements.

Two major considerations play a role in world futuring. The first is the ever-present progressive aspiration to achieve world government. Listen to how George Soros and Barack Obama clearly articulate this notion. Both desire the lessening of national identities along with a world without borders or nations, and with a single centralized government.

The second consideration involves what may be perceived as the early steps toward the establishment of a progressive world order. The European Union is an example of this. It can be seen as the early efforts to accomplish world government although it's scope is currently limited to European trading partners. The European Union is perhaps the most ambitious and most successful example of peaceful international cooperation in world history. Starting out with good intentions, it was designed to be an organization where one country helps another in a common bond that provided security and economic strength. However, the corrosive influences of progressive ideology and racketeerism have transformed it into a danger to freedom.

History of the European Union

The development of a unified Europe has long been an objective of Western civilization. In the past, there have been numerous attempts to establish such an order. Forms of unity were developed in times of ancient Rome, the Byzantium, the Holy Roman Empire, and the Ottoman Empire. More recently, even the designs of Nazi Germany can be seen as an attempt to achieve centralized control of Europe.

The horror of world war led to the creation of the International Coal & Steel Commission (ECSC), which was an attempt on the part of European countries to control the materials used to manufacture instruments of war. The European Union later arose from the early beginnings of the ECSC. Today the European Union represents the economic and political union of twenty-seven independent member states enjoying liberalized trade. It coordinates its economic policies through centralized decision-making in a Brussels headquarters rather than in individual national capitals. European citizens of member states have overwhelmingly expressed approval of their country's decision to join the union. The majority of citizens (56 percent) believes that membership of the EU has benefited their country, though a significant minority (31 percent) does not agree.

National vs. Supranational

You might expect some tension between the autonomy of individual member states and the structure of centralized control of a supranational entity. Some of the trappings of national identity are gone. When you live in the EU you don't need a passport to go from one country to another. Seventeen member states have the same currency, the Euro. The European Union has its own flag and even its own anthem ("Ode to Joy").

It is really quite a challenge to understand how the European Union works with its councils, commission and parliament, and the presidents of each member state. The bottom line is that what started out as an effort to develop an open market has transformed into a federal state, a supranational entity.

Supranationalism—a form of organization through which decisions are made by international institutions, not by individual states.

> **Intergovernmental: a form of international organization where governments work together to achieve shared goals.**

The European Union and lack of democracy

The characteristic of this state is that it suffers from a democratic deficit. According to Soviet dissident Vladimir Bukovsky, the lack of representation is not unintentional. Rather it reflects the ideological goals of left-wing parties of Europe and the former Soviet Union: "We are living in a period of rapid, systemic and very consistent dismantlement of democracy."

Bukovsky related to Paul Belien how the events in Europe in 1985–86 drove Italian Communists and German Social Democrats to a meeting with Gorbachev. The group was reeling from the Thatcher-led movement toward privatization and economic liberalization. "Wild capitalization" threatened to reverse the achievements of generations of Socialists and Social Democrats. The new plan was to make a worldwide effort to install identical socialist goals in all countries at once.

1985, was a turning point for left-wing parties and the Soviet Union

Before 1985, left-wing parties perceived European integration as an obstacle to Socialist goals and opposed it. After 1985, they embraced it and worked together to hijack the common market project and put it on the road to becoming a totalitarian state. While the collapse of the Soviet Union left only the European part of the plan in effect, Socialist goals expanded into the United States. Notice the intricate parallels between the Socialist-Communist reaction to privatization in the 1980s and that of the Obama administration's 2012 call to transfer wealth from the more successful Americans. This was done in unity with the various Soros-financed organizations participating in the Occupy Wall Street movement. All three reactions are expression of the common goal to undermine capitalism.

The Alinsky attack truth

By now, readers will have little trouble in detecting the Alinsky attack truth in the progressive developments of the European Union. We start off with the truth that we are the world; we are the people. We need to coexist in peace, and therefore international cooperation of some form is vital for this purpose. Negotiating away trade barriers allows the free flow of goods and services to the benefit of mankind.

Even the concept of internationalism, as a political movement, has merit. Internationalists advocate a greater economic and political cooperation among nations for the benefit of all, and it should be noted that internationalism is not necessarily antinationalism. It espouses an appreciation of diverse culture and a desire for world peace. Logically, internationalism is opposed to the radical nationalism that created the ferments that resulted in Imperial Japan and Nazi Germany.

But internationalists are also advocates of international organizations, which predisposes them to support a world government.

Bukovsky warns that the European Union is a program for the obliteration of nation states. This is, of course, consistent with the ideology of NeoGeo discussed earlier and also with Obama's brand of foreign policy, inasmuch as he wants America to eschew the role of a distinguished superpower, preferring instead that the United States submerse itself into European efforts such as we saw in the NATO response in the Libyan uprising.

How the EU Government Works to Control Europe

The European Union government is based on a series of five treaties dating back to 1957. In 2003 the union made a bid for a constitution that would replace the treaties; France and the Netherlands voted it down. The 2007 Lisbon Treaty was designed to do what the constitution bid would have done, namely, to establish the European Union as the official government of Europe. Ireland rejected Lisbon; a huge controversy developed when a second referendum was presented to the Irish people, who voted no in 2009.

The Lisbon Treaty passage increases the democratic deficit of the European Union, making the unelected commission and its president the most powerful EU body. As a result of Lisbon, the commissioner derives his executive power from the treaties alone, whereas formerly the executive power was held by the European Council, which conferred those powers on the commission. The Council is comprised of the heads of state of member nations. As Bukovsky describes it, the European commission resembles the Politburo of the Soviet- "…they are… unaccountable to anyone, not directly elected by anyone at all." They are exactly the same.

Futuring

According to our scenario, the European Union will pursue the NeoGeo effort to squelch national identity of member countries and we will have a counterpart of this in the United States as the Obama administration furthers programs to do the same. The United States and European nations will have the absolute concept of their constitutions undermined by pragmatism and the furthering of the Soros philosophy that collective interests transcend state boundaries. The Obama appointment of transnational advisors Harold Koh and Eric Schwartz will further the subordination of American criminal justice procedures to International Criminal Court rulings in a number of cases.

CHAPTER 28

Ireland and the European Union

Ireland, a tiny country with a population of under 4.5 million, 87 percent Roman Catholic, is another country in the throes of a DRAG recession, with an unemployment rate of 12.5 percent. There is probably no better example of how an EU member gets hammered by the agenda of an increasingly totalitarian federal superstate ideology than Ireland.

Look at how Ireland voted no on the Treaty of Niece only to have it reappear in the guise of the Treaty of Lisbon. Again the Irish people voted no. It didn't matter how they voted. They would simply have to vote again. And again. Until they voted yes. That's how the relentless progressive agenda of the European Union operates.

The Lisbon Treaty was designed to replace a previous failed attempt to wrap the EU member states in a constitution that would replace all treaties. Lisbon was the most recent attempt to make citizens of European nations citizens of the EU.

The fundamental problem lies in the fact that a constitution, like the US Constitution, should reflect the people it purports to govern. The would be EU plan mirrors no such population.

The French social philosopher Alexis de Tocqueville visited the United States in an attempt to study the stability of modern democratic federal states. What made it work, he noted, was "the slowly evolving cultural disposition for self government, a common system of law, language and religion." All of these are lacking among EU nations. The Irish people with their overwhelming majority of Catholic representation reject abortion. Yet the Irish were forced to vote on a second referendum on the Treaty of Lisbon. This time they voted yes with a 67 percent majority. Why?

In the first place, one might ask why they had to vote on a treaty they had already rejected. In fact, why should any EU country have to vote again on a treaty they have rejected? The answer is that the EU leadership does not represent a highly innovative, brilliant group open to new concepts and ways of solving problems for the European Community. Rather it is a totalitarian operation, hell-bent on a very limited agenda that it has no intention of abandoning. The Irish leaders capitulated under pressure from international groups and other EU countries to submit to the referendum. The new treaty referendum included certain concessions to the Irish people—legal guarantees regarding sovereignty, taxes, the military, and family matters, including abortion. In addition, the Irish found themselves in the severity of an economic downturn, and the financial benefits of further EU involvement were especially enticing to the growing number of unemployed youths.

The Irish previously rejected the Lisbon Treaty with a majority of 53.4 percent, but in 2009, they accepted with a majority of 67 percent. Then in December of 2010, the Irish people got quite a jolt: **EU Court Orders Ireland to Scrap Anti-Abortion Laws**.

That is how the headlines read. Actually the judgment was from the European Court of Human Rights, which is not officially part of the EU system. However, the EU Court of Justice refers to case law of the Court of Human Rights.

At issue in the ruling was the right of women to have an abortion in life-threatening situations. In 1992, the Irish Supreme Court declared that abortion should be legal when a woman's life is at stake. The Irish government did not enact legislation to affect current laws, claiming that abortion in those circumstances is done anyway. Irish Minister of Public Health Mary Harney advised that changing abortion laws "will take some time as it is a highly sensitive and complex area."

Notice what is happening here: rulings of EU-associated courts can affect legislation in Ireland on a matter of social sensitivity and certainly religious faith. The Irish as a people are opposed to abortion. The EU treaty made a concession on this part, but an international court made an attack on their social order.

It's reasonable to suspect that this is only the beginning.. Subsequent rulings could affect all aspects of life, including the education of children, especially in regard to matters of religious faith and sexuality. What we have not yet got around to is the ability of international courts to enforce their orders.

Futuring

By 2020, Ireland will be one of the countries that elects a unilateral withdrawal from the European Union. This will be in response to aggressive enforcement of EU unity in social matters, but it will also be a response to the lagging Irish economy with a GDP that will never be sufficient to allow repayment of EU-negotiated loans.

CHAPTER 29

US-EU Legal Parity

There are two things every American needs to know about the European Union's expansion into the legal system. First, it enacts laws and rulings that control the lives of millions of Europeans and does so without any real electoral representation. Furthermore it does this by the power of socialist elites, including supporters of the former Soviet Union.

The second thing to know that it's coming right to you, courtesy of the same Socialist elites, right on your doorstep, right into your home to dictate how your family will live.

Look at how it works for Europe. The law of the European Union results from proposals put forth by the Commission. This is the EU body that the Lisbon Treaty made the most powerful unit in the entire EU system. Who appoints members to the commission? That's an excellent question. The governments of EU member nations appoint them, but without consent of the electorate, and often it is a political decision influenced by other nations. Look at the flack the British government received when it appointed Baroness Catherine Ashton as UK commissioner. The British government was highly criticized for allowing the French government to enforce Ashton as their choice for Britain when more favorable candidates appeared to be available.

Six minutes of representation.

In order for laws prepared by the commission to take effect, they must be approved by the Council of Ministers and the European Parliament.

The sole representative of the people in the entire EU system "usually gets to speak for about 6 minutes a year."

The European Parliament is the only directly elected body, in the whole process, yet the voter turnout for the candidate for the member of the European Parliament (MEP) is usually quite low. Bukovsky notes how this sole representative of the people in the entire EU system "can speak for 6 minutes per year in the Chamber." The President of the European Parliament is elected by a process monopolized by two leading parties that have worked out a system, whereby they take turns so they divide the rule Parliament up between them.

Now it seems pretty reasonable that a trade organization of any kind needs to enact laws. An international entity like the European Union has legitimate cause to pass a law, say, allowing oranges from southern Italy to be sold in a market in Holland. But the EU law goes beyond that: it has expanded into criminal codes and, as we saw in the case of Ireland, it intrudes into matters of religion and family life.

There is some concern that laws passed by the EU commission could affect US law. Not surprisingly, progressives have taken aim at any resistance to the notion that international laws should not be brought to bear on the United States. They claim such resistance is a "dangerous myth."

Consider the typical progressive lineup of jargon used in Anne Marie Slaughter's 2005 diatribe (pre-Lisbon.) Any objections to accepting internationalization of US laws are: an "oversimplification", "hyperbolic", "deeply worrying", "irresponsible", "dangerous", " inaccurate", "naïve", "unsupported claims." All of the preceding were issued within the space of a few paragraphs. Notice how the progressive mind-set always works with the same poverty of intelligence. Slaughter resurrects the history of jingoism and the most extreme cases of radical nationalism to serve as a barrier to any criticism of the European Union's destruction of cultural and religious values.

What Americans should be concerned about

An area of particular concern to Americans is the promulgation of "human rights" into EU law. Hate speech, racial offenses, and criticism of the European Union are lumped together into a gigantic movement to squelch opposition to the EU agenda. In the European Union, offensive speech is now considered a criminal act, even if what one says is true. In the United States there is for now a guarantee of freedom of speech: one is free to speak the truth regardless of whose feelings are hurt. School children used to be taught this basic principle in American History classes, where they learned about the Alien and Sedition Acts of 1798. This act ended the common law precedent of the time and allowed truth as a defense against libel or sedition (badmouthing the powers that be).

Publisher John Peter Zenger was arrested and imprisoned for seditious libel in 1734 after his newspaper criticized the colonial governor of New York. Zenger spent nearly ten months in jail before being acquitted by a jury in August 1735.

Contrast that with the March 6, 2001 case, *Connolly* v. *Commission,* that was shamelessly decided by the European Court of Justice. Connolly sued the Commission because he was deprived of employment and revenues for publishing an exposé of misconduct at the European Union. The commission and EU court found that Connolly may or may not have made false or misleading accusations in his criticism of the EU monetary regulation. They made no effort to prove that his allegations were false. (They were in fact true.) The fact that they were critical of the European Union, that is to say the EU's image suffered, was sufficient to bring a decision against Connolly.

European Union reverses centuries of fundamental liberties

The *Connolly* decision, in contrast to Zenger's case, was justified on the very grounds **that Connolly's content made the European Union look bad**. Thus the European Union reverses centuries of fundamental liberties and essentially reestablishes the injustice of the crime of seditious libel. And Anne Marie Slaughter thinks you are "irresponsible" and "dangerous" should you be at all concerned about this tyranny coming soon to a courthouse near you.

We have already seen the Obama administration faithfully installing the beginnings of seditious libel. We saw it in Axelrod's allegations about the nature of Fox News. It's a turn around approach to eroding the freedom of speech. In all his prattle, Axelrod was unable to deliver a single fragment of Fox not telling the truth. To put it straight up: Fox could criticize the Obama administration because it could defend itself with the truth. Otherwise Obama could gleefully and successfully sue. In his statement Axelrod was not merely whining, as some have suggested. He actually espoused a very important principle in both Alinsky and Lenin political theory.

In the Alinsky framework, he attempted to neutralize the truth about Obama and company by rendering Fox as the subject of controversy. Was it a news channel or not? That's fodder for endless debate, to be sure. The question took attention away from what Fox actually said. But what about the strategy pronounced by Lenin in his powerful work "Who Rules?" Lenin taught that one needs to eliminate criticism of a program because such criticism allows for the introduction of a new outside agenda. I refer to this joint action to simultaneously eliminate freedom of the press and block the introduction of a non-party agenda as Axelrodianism.

Futuring

Based on the above observations, we predict that the legal structure of the United States will become heavily influenced by the EU associated courts of justice and human rights certainly by 2016. Seditious libel will be reinstated as a criminal act, and violation of hate speech laws will become commonplace charges against a variety of citizens. These laws will develop into all forms reflecting political correctness that Obama's new militia will enforce.

CHAPTER 30

Tyranny of the European Union

In a January 2003 issue of *The Economist*, an article entitled "Tyranny of the Tiny" argued that in the European Union it is the smalls that have the advantage. The article pointed out that each central bank has equal voice in the management of economic policy. German Bundesbank and Greek Central Bank equally control decisions on EU financial policy.

Most of the people of the EU live in only six nations. Decisions are made by all member nations by proportionate vote. In one country 80,000 votes are enough to elect a member of the European Parliament, whereas in another country with a larger population a representative may need 800,000.

The article is somewhat misleading in that it fails to point out that smaller states are at a much greater risk of loss of independence. Larger nations are definitely able to exert pressure on smaller countries. Consider, for example, the case of the British prime minister putting pressure on Ireland as part of the EU's bullying Ireland to hold referendums despite voting no previously. The disadvantage of the small will quickly appear with EU enforcement. The commission, as already pointed out, has the power to use the force of member nations as well as its own agencies to enforce legislation, but the larger nations are the ones that provide the military and political muscle of the EU. The possibility clearly exists for a smaller country to find its soil occupied by an extranational force.

Inbred Coerciveness.

There is in a certain sense an amount of inbred coerciveness that is required in any organization, especially something like the European Union. Every organization has to have rules. It is even suggested that the European Union does not have enough control of member states to effectively carry out legitimate activities. In a recent statement, Jack Delors, who was the founding architect of the single European currency, the euro, agreed with Britain when they objected to adopting it. They claimed that the currency could not work without a single European state. Britain declined to adopt the euro as their currency and retained the pound instead.

More recently, German Prime Minister Angela Merkel has expressed the necessity of finding a way to control countries' expenditures in order to get some kind of the order in the European Union. Left to their own devices, member countries show a lack of fiscal responsibility, racking up big debts to the detriment of all member nations.

Antidemocratic features

As mentioned earlier, the provisions of the Treaty of Lisbon have introduced some fairly undemocratic features into the EU leadership. The appointment of the commission is an example. The forcing of repeat voting on endless reformations is certainly not characteristic of democratic society. Why should a no vote not be accepted the first time? Continuing the voting until they get the desired results means that a member's vote doesn't really count; it means leadership didn't really want input. When the EU leadership gets the results they want, the voting stops. Why should it stop? Shouldn't it be an annual thing if that's the precedent set?

In a 2006 interview, Victor Bukovsky predicted that the European Union would design hate speech laws and enforce them against anyone who disagrees with the EU agenda or violates political correctness and therefore receives the label of racist. He drew a parallel between the European Union's upcoming facilities for the imprisonment of violators of political correctness that will develop, and the psychiatric institutions that he endured in Soviet Union in the '60s and '70s.

It is interesting to note that the new Socialist president of the European Union, Martin Schulz, has stressed the "mental weakness" of Eurosceptics (critics the European Union.) Schulz is a strong believer in the abolition of nation states.

We noted that parliament was the only electorally based unit in the European Union, but the fact that the average member of parliament gets only six minutes a year to speak in chamber lends credibility to Bukovsky's assertion that the body is not a real parliament.

Forecast

There will be increased EU aggression to enforce associated court decisions affecting the culture and life of member states. European Union legislation will extend into abortion and child's rights legislation as well as the freedom of religion and climate-energy regulation.

Hate crimes and seditious libel charges will end freedom of speech. Racketeering will fund the establishment of an *apparat-chik* among Brussels' leadership. There will be a push of a denationalization agenda. Religious and family life values will suffer increasing attacks in the name of "human rights." Further discussion of these factors and the defection of states and financial difficulties are the subject of the next chapter.

CHAPTER 31

June 2018—The Collapse of the European Union

Imagine for a moment you are part of a family in which your father works hard to bring home a paycheck. But one day he tells you and the rest of your family that he has to give the paycheck to people living in the next town. Sorry about your not having all the wonderful things you like to have in life; it's got to go to the next town. Why? Because someone in that town wants to have money to go to school. Another neighbor wants to retire, and another man made bad investments and wants to be bailed out. So everyone on your block has to pay for all these people you've never met in the next town. Worse, as days go by, it seems they require more and more money out of your family's pocket.

Citizens of many countries in the European Union are beginning to find themselves in the same situation as the above family. Because of fundamental weaknesses and imbalances of member-state economies, there is pressure to bail these weaker members out of their financial crisis.

Popularity of the European Union

Is it possible that the overwhelming popularity the European Union has enjoyed may finally be coming to an end? The rise of a Finn political party critical of EU bailouts of member states may be a sign of this. The True Finns, a nationalist oriented party, represents a major political force in Finland.

As already noted one of the planners behind the concept of a single European currency, Jacques Delors, said that euro zone was flawed from the beginning. Without some kind of central control to regulate economic policies, individual members could run up unsustainable debt. Politicians in the EU countries had control of heavy government borrowing from banks and entities, including various European stability funds. The proceeds from these loans went to the European central banks, who in turn made an increasing number of loans to the politicians, who began the borrowing process anew.

Financial corruption

Daniel Hannan in *The Telegraph* back in 2007 reported on the corruption in the European Union itself. He mentioned that the Court of Auditors had not once signed off on a budget, as provided by law. He noted that millions of euro dollars earmarked for support of farms ended up financing golfing clubs and that 60 percent of the budget failed to meet approval. Aside from the antidemocratic ideology driving the European Union, the enterprise functions as a racket to distribute wealth to EU principles.

Breakup scenarios

As problems in member states like Greece capture headlines with violent rioting in response to government fiscal control, some have wondered whether the European Union might eventually decide to lop off weaker members.

The possibility of withdrawing from the EU. Has any country ever done it?

The Lisbon Treaty states that a country's decision to withdraw from the European Union should be respected. In a very real sense, the country retains its autonomy. Have there been any withdrawals from the EU in the past?

Certain territories, such as Greenland separated from the European Union when they gained their independence from Denmark in 2008. The same applied to Algiers.

But there's no provision for *suspending* a member country, only for voluntary withdrawal. Lopping off of Greece would be unprecedented. Moreover, countries leaving the European Union for any reason would be a challenge to the concept of internationalist ideology. It frustrates the plan for a one-world government. For that reason internationalists such as the Trilateral Commission and others move in with some form of financing.

Problems arise from this approach to sustaining countries through EU efforts. The German constitution explicitly forbids EU bailouts. With worsening economic conditions, there'll be pressure on Germany to abandon this absolute position.

EU dictatorship in action

But what happens if a country is sustaining really big economic setbacks and uses EU-arranged financing to borrow increasingly large amounts and then decides to quit? Timo Soini, leader of the True Finns political party notes,

"Unfortunately for this financial and political cartel, their plan isn't working. Already under the scheme, Greece, Ireland and Portugal are in ruins. They will never be able to save and grow fast enough to pay back the debts which Brussels has saddled them in the name of saving them."

The Lisbon treaty has provisions for bilateral withdrawal from the European Union, but what will happen if a country with a sizable debt decides to leave and renege on all that debt? Will the European Union take coercive measures? If a country like Ireland, for example, sees that there's no way its GDP could ever allow it to liquidate debts, it might consider taking such steps—especially if it were able to partner with countries with new opportunities for trade, those the NeoGeo economy. Deals with developing countries, including Brazil and India, with participation in Pacific Basin Growth all dwarf the advantages of EU trade with its sluggish European markets.

The likelihood of coercive internationalism is not restricted to finance. We have seen that the European Union has an agenda regarding almost all aspects of human life. Associated courts are beginning to make decisions regarding family matters, energy, climate, and education. They all impact the country's decision to escape EU control. Individual nations may decide that government oppression is not worth safety and security.

We predict that there will be some attempt by the European Union to enforce progressive ideology. The attempt to enforce human rights edicts will take effect through both EU agencies and the manipulation of units of member nations. This oppression, combined with financial problems, will lead to the collapse of the European Union. For that reason we predict that, upon collapse, the President and Members of the Commission of the EU will be arrested and tried as war criminals for injuries suffered in enforcing progressive court mandates in member nations.

Commentary: Why did the European Union fail?

Did this extraordinary aspiration of peaceful unity among nations really collapse due to lack of financial discipline, or was the corrosive influence of progressive ideology the deciding factor?

In the news and analysis posting in the *Daily Bell*, the authors note how the empires of Central and South America are so often touted on the History Channel for their greatness and culture. The *Bell* authors suggest that the real story of greatness starts with the city-states that gave rise to the Empire. This is the true source of the rich culture history admires. The Empire was not the beginning of greatness, but rather the end. The ever greater and more powerful empires, with their endless warfare and bloodletting, created a horrible existence. Their atrocities sowed the seeds for their own destruction. How did these empires end? They ended not with a bang but with a whimper. The people had enough and merely blended back into the jungles.

This seems to fittingly forecast the fate of the European Union, a slower unraveling, a steady retreat of countries into national identity and individual freedom.

Futuring

In the period between 2017 and 2018, the European Union will decline and then collapse, resulting in a short-lived rise in the value of the dollar.

PART SEVEN

Reemergence of Representation

CHAPTER 32

Decoupled Economics

As the European Union struggles to survive, other countries will be showing more resilience to global economic downturns. This gives rise to the concept of decoupling or two-speed economies mentioned elsewhere. In the West, the economy remains fragile while the East—Asia, Africa, and the Middle East—and Latin America have shown greater increase in GDP.

As of 2012, problems in the United States and Europe appear to be primarily financial. We talked about the US debt overhang and the declining US dollar, which together prevent anything but a meager real GDP in the neighborhood of 2 percent. The European Union is facing the failure of Soviet style central banking, a decrease in the value of the euro, and a sluggish economy. Poor financial control of member nations' growing debt plays a large factor in this.

This brings us to the countries that are referred to as the emerging economy, the real place to look for growth.

Consider India, which is Asia's third-largest economy. It has a growth rate of 7.4 percent annually. The average GDP for all African countries rose from 3.1 percent in 2009 to 4.9 percent in 2010. What drives growth in these countries?

Gerald Lyons of *Commodities Now*, suggests the following: First, there is a middle class appearing on the scene that brings about a need for products for consumer market. Infrastructure investments also play a role. Such investment requires financing from various parties, both foreign and domestic. A very important part of networking for emerging markets is the opening of "New Trade Corridors." All this development becomes more of a reality with a decrease in the corruption indices for the respective governments, a factor that previously hindered growth.

Western economists view the growth in emerging markets as a catch-up pattern, meaning that the various GDPs show growth above trend expectations for now but will slow with export growth. Presently, the reported trend exceeds economic experts' expectation of below 6.3 percent. When the markets mature, they will decrease to a 3 percent rate of annual growth. Lyons suggests that "no region is fully decoupled from events elsewhere." Therefore economic boom in the East and Latin America will, according to most experts, drive recovery in the West. As China gets back to an increase in GDP, it will pull up the worldwide economy. We will review these assumptions in a later chapter.

The situation in Africa

Africa is a region that has pulled ahead in GDP, rising to 6.8 percent in West Africa and 6.7 percent in East Africa in 2010 despite the trouble revealed in headlines that continue to report strife in Libya and the Ivory Coast and despite the fact that a big African trading partner, Japan, endured an extremely severe earthquake in 2009.

"Africa is indeed moving from vision to action," the South African financial minister told Bloomberg's Nasheen Sevik. Factors that help Africa move ahead include economic policies that provide a cushion for problems with food harvests. But population in Africa is increasing, and unemployment, especially among the young is a problem.

China has replaced the United States as Africa's biggest trading partner, but the States and the European Union remain still the biggest financial sources through Foreign Direct Investment

(FDI) and Official Development Assistance (ODA.) However, the new emerging market partners are coming up with fast-growing, innovative financing programs. As we'll see, some of these new financing concepts empowering the developing economies will introduce two unexpected results. The first is that it will involve individual US citizens as direct investors. The second, much to the surprise of Western economic experts, is that the new concepts will allow emerging market countries to pursue an unprecedented trend in their pattern of growth.

CHAPTER 33

February 2018— The US Society and Progressive Decline

At this point (in 2018) we return to US society, now having experienced almost a decade of progressive rule. Unlike the 2000-days scenario, the period considered here covers a more pliable timeline; it may extend into 2030 and even beyond.

The economy is going to experience a prolonged, slow growth after a spurt that occurs early in 2013. By 2020, the US economy, while still huge, will be down to 20 percent the size of the pre-Obama levels. An increased number of failed government investments in green economy along with unsuccessful US competition in global markets will account for this. Watch the Super Bowl ads running from 2013 to 2018. You'll find that there will be a steady decrease in advertising, and the ads that do appear will be increasingly less spectacular.

Our scenario predicts a credit market collapse, bringing about increased use of cash in the US economy, and with it an increased crime rate is predicted. To offset this, a new financial institution will arise—the small-scale currency-backed exchanges (CBE), which, as the name indicates, backs its reserves with currencies of nations that have rising GDPs. By 2017 the government will enact various laws to control the flow of cash, particularly at airports. Currency-backed exchanges will help to alleviate this situation. When Americans get their paychecks, they will immediately convert into another currency as it's deposited into the currency-backed exchanges. This will enable efficient deployment of funds for foreign investment. Government attempts to control currency exchange will meet with enormous resistance from minorities and international organizations, causing governments to back off.

The culture of a post-2016 US society will be determined by the *apparatchik.* Increased policing of the workplace for political correctness and control of school programs by separate federal entities will be part of the landscape.

Elimination of religious expression

For the Catholic faithful, the final eradication of genuine religious expression in public will occur by 2017. The most serious issue leading to this will involve homosexual practices. The passing of the Freedom of Sex Act of 2015 will force all organizations performing marriages to include ceremonies for same-sex couples. One can easily predict the reaction of the Catholic Church membership to such a mandate. Catholics will splinter. The official Church will quietly withdraw from performing marriages in public. Some pastors, however, will cooperate, embracing the *Real Katolique.* Theologians will deemphasize the role of the Church in marriage. "After all," they will say, referring to orthodox teaching, "the real minister of marriage is not the priest, but the marrying couple. The only reason why the Church is involved in marriage is because Jesus in the Gospels showed up at a wedding. "If Jesus had showed up at childbirth," they'll say, "the Church would make all us priests midwives. And God forbid if he had showed up at a circumcision!"

Following the *Real Katolique,* public marriage in the Church will denigrate into a sort of public blessing ceremony—"We bring animals into the church for the blessing of St. Francis, don't we? Why can't we do it for all?" The true Roman Catholic Church will never participate and will forbid the practice of blessing homosexual unions.

Progressive rulings will not only affect marriages: many Church teachings on sexuality that are not politically correct will be interpreted as hate speech punishable by law. Catholic marriage and instruction will therefore be conducted in secret, mostly in homes of the faithful. Some priests will be betrayed and be subjected to fines and/or imprisonment by the progressive government.

Pilgrimages to foreign countries will become popular for Catholic couples, particularly to Mexico, which will be a favorite site for weddings. Returning home, Catholics may undergo a civil ceremony, but the issuance of marriage certificates must be accompanied by an approval for childbirth, which will force many Catholics and their young families to "live in the shadows."

The availability of health care for all will mean the government will be involved in everyone's health practices. The core of the Obama plan, in conjunction with the Jaffee Memorandum, will be the woman's reproductive capacity. The first oppressive measure to come about will be mandated abortions. At first these will be justified by some medical reason, but eventually the medical necessity will be marginal, leaving many confused by the practice. All universities and all health care facilities involved in the care of women must adopt the Sebelius Principle, namely that the science of women's reproduction is defined by the statements of Health and Human Services to the effect that the availability of contraception and abortion has been shown to improve women's health. The publication of any other reports or studies purported as science that are contrary to this provision will be a crime punishable by fine and imprisonment.

In accordance with the Planned Parenthood Memo, all schoolchildren will be instructed in reproductive control and the value of a decreased carbon footprint in their own lives and the lives of their parents, whom they will be required to monitor daily for reportable violations. Sterilization and euthanasia will likewise be promoted. While the suicide rate among preteens has tripled since the 1970s, for the first time the nation will be seeing a sustained high level of suicide among first graders.

Problems at the US southern borders will worsen. In accordance with the progressive ideology, no effort will be made to stem the tide of illegal immigration or the transport of drugs. Efforts by border states to infringe on the immigration flow will be challenged in federal courts. Drug cartels will flourish, along with staggering increases in the number of public murders of both US and Mexico citizens.

Consolidation of Hispanic population

With the achievement of citizenship, members of the Hispanic population will become increasingly assertive and more vocal in their criticism of progressive power. The law mandating diversity in the workplace will not affect many Hispanic businesses. This will also encourage an increase in cash-only business transactions. The passage of the Dream Act will provide educational opportunities for Hispanics, and there will be some continuation of financial programs for the Occupy Homes offshoot of the Occupy Wall Street movement, but this will decline substantially over time.

The Arc Declines.

The US government will find itself facing a decrease in revenue and, starting in 2017, a decrease in popularity. More than 75 percent of the US population will view progressive rule unfavorably by 2018. By then Obama's 2012 and 2016 statements of concern for sharing of wealth will be revealed as a sham. The new *apparatchik* that develops as a privileged class separate from the masses will very likely include leading Republicans that will choose to adopt membership in the new class in order to preserve their careers and class status.

A big problem for the government will be its inability to enforce its progressive measures in everyday life due to growing resistance and hatred of militia. Presidential speeches will be boycotted by most viewing audiences. The president's attempt to make public appearances will be severely limited due to security troubles and sparse crowd turnout.

Ethnic tension will develop but this time not between the races but rather between minorities and the government. As result of progressive materialism and anti-transcendence measures voiding public expression of religion, the Hispanic and other ethnic populations will develop into a very potent political force against progressive ideology.

The population will be subjected to endless referendums, but the results will be misrepresented; eventually voter turnout will decline substantially.

Regionalism—the most serious challenge to the Obama progressive regime

Regionalism was actually an unintended but important consequence of jettisoning the Electoral College system. By replacing the Electoral College with the popular referendum, the Obama progressive party reintroduced a problem that had long ago been remedied by the prior federal system, namely, how can all states have their interests adequately represented regardless of their population size? The smaller states now find themselves hopelessly left out of the new scheme of things.

But a solution is at hand. The tiny states find they are able to ally themselves with some states, such as Texas, that have sizable, expanding populations and nurture a conflict of their own with the increasingly dictatorial nature of the Washington institution. The federal government has become increasingly reluctant to deal with Southern border issues, particularly those resulting from frequent drug-traffic-related violence. Besides, the progressive ideology espouses the NeoGeo premise of a world order without border restrictions. As a result of the federal absence, the border states have become increasingly powerful and are able to check actions of the green militia and other segments of the national force that attempt to occupy their states. They have actually taken steps to eliminate possible federal control, including the emptying of the National Guard official register. They deliberately ensured that no available facilities would meet GSA standards for federal government offices. The workers were even denied amenities in first-class hotels, where laundry "mistakes" left representatives of the progressive regime walking around squishing in excrement-laden underwear as they attempted to carry out Obama's regulations. Relief-seeking Americans from all over the country flocked to these militia-restricted zones.

Believing that the national militia would be sufficient to control a cowering, financially beleaguered citizenry, the Obama team committed the armed forces to services under foreign leadership, preferring to integrate their activities with international organizations such as NATO, the United Nations, and the European Union. But faced with resistance in southern states, the progressive rulers began to extricate forces from foreign control; this proved to be a slow and tedious process.

It may turn out that—in responding to progressive tyranny, a border-state governor, such as Perry, can play a far more important role in American history than he ever would have as the Republican nominee for president.

In reference to the twelve steps presented earlier, the population in this period will have passed through devastation and aimlessness and have begun to climb toward supremacy, moving through nesting and networking. The next chapter will introduce a dazzling innovation.

CHAPTER 34

Unrepatriated Profits

Nine-year-old Patricia Childs sits at her computer enthusiastically involved in conversation with an online playmate. What makes this remarkable is that she actually has a young girl on speaker, and the child's British accent fills the apartment. Patricia belongs to an online Penguin club, a closely monitored program that allows children all over the world to contact each other daily. Using Skype, there is no cost for the phone call. Earlier in the day, the nine-year-old spoke to a girl from France. But what if the French girl was unable to speak English? No problem. There are free online programs that make available rapid translation of languages so Patricia could even speak in Chinese to a friend in Asia.

This tremendous increase in the use of computer technology at all age levels has permitted traffic between different peoples in a revolutionary way that has not been witnessed since Augustine's Pax Romana and the construction of Roman highways throughout the Mediterranean countries.

Shoes second; Microsoft first

It is been said that while most of the world's population goes without shoes and basic sanitation, those situations will be remedied much later than the problem of going without a computer.

Computers will come first. Imagine other innovations that may occur as a result of this growing personal contact among individuals throughout the world. Keeping in mind the separation of development arcs and the fact that emerging market countries are moving faster than those of the United States or Europe, imagine what is going on with parents of all the children Patricia is in contact with almost daily.

One father may be a farmer in the West Indies who finds that every time he shows up at market he quickly sells out of his melons and wishes he had more produce to offer. An investment in a truck would allow him to transport more than his donkey cart allows—both more of his own fruit and maybe that of his neighbors who are unable to take the time and expense to travel to markets some distance away. Then there's a young housewife called Nokia in Central Africa who wants to work at home with her children. She found a demand for clothing that she designs and produces with a borrowed sewing machine. She thinks about how much more she could make if she were able to get hold of a dozen sewing machines and put young girls in her village to work on her designs. An unemployed law school graduate in Brazil believes the he is able to find properties he could easily renovate and sell at a tremendous price to the new generation of consumers in the growing economy of his country.

A new breed of banking—the NanoBank

All of these situations would be largely ignored by local banking establishments, if the banks even existed in the vicinity of these potential entrepreneurs. Enter a new breed of banking—the NanoBank.

The NanoBank uses the ubiquity of computer technology and the ability to make overseas contact at a personal level through a specially designed network, a carefully monitored "Penguin Club" for mom-and-pop investors.

In the United States, in order for trust funds and investment portfolios to meet requirements of retirement programs, they need an 8 percent return rate (on average). And what did we say was the US current yield? They can is barely eke out a 2 percent return, which means that for many Americans, their retirement is in question. The NanoBank allows participation in deals in which the average annual return would easily be 20 percent and perhaps even a great deal more. What is even more attractive is that if American investors decide to leave their money in the account in local currency and not repatriate any profits, the funds are tax free. And as the dollar devalues, investors see their funds rise in value or maintain stability since they are the currencies in demand in the real financial market. The deals may seem small, but in terms of the number of deals a NanoBank can put together, they could easily number in the millions. And in dollar amounts, we are talking billions.

American investors in the "Post-2000 Day Era" may have an additional motivation in participating in nanobanking, namely that it deprives the government of revenue and therefore control of their lives. The progressive government changes will have created considerable resentment in most Americans. The population impact phase discussed in earlier chapters has now turned from devastation to decisive action in the direction of increased freedom. If you're looking at having to continue to work for another ten years and want to have enough to retire, you might be more than willing to consider investing overseas and living on a very limited income while the investment grows without taxation. One of the benefits is that you could visit the country of your holdings and vacation tax free.

The main question, of course, would center on the risk of these transactions handled by nano professionals in question, but self-regulation will quickly develop in this area to maintain investment opportunities. Like other markets, standards must be clearly enunciated, and any violations will be severely punished.

Impact of NanoBanks on the United States

The effect of nanobanking on the United States is obvious. It provides an additional constraint on a government that has overspent in the amount of trillions. At first the progressive government will attempt to restrict nanobanking. It will attempt to control online activity. But the decades of cloud computing by the government makes them more vulnerable to control by hackers, exerting more pressure on the government than they could ever exert on the general population.

An additional factor in controlling government interference stems from the China bank. The Chinese government desires to restore the valuable American consumer market. China will inform the United States that any attempts to increase new money supply by Fiat will be met with a flood of US debentures on the financial markets, thereby dramatically decreasing the value of new debt offerings by the United States.

New growth pattern for the emergent economies

World economists will begin to realize that they made a serious mistake in assessing Third-World catch-up scenarios. Their expectation was that the Third World would follow the pattern seen in Western countries.

Real vs. virtual economy

Adrian Salbuchi makes a distinction between two types of economies that have largely figured into Western development and led to the financial crisis. The Real Economy is based on work. "And work is what runs the planet Earth: you need work, talent and effort to build new cars or airplanes or clothes or new homes or roads; work to bake more bread and harvest more food."

In contrast to this is the Virtual Economy, namely the world of finance, the one that uses "virtual numbers, fraudulent derivatives, casino-like speculative investments." The Virtual Economy is essentially parasitic living off of the real economy.

A more balanced view would show that derivatives are not necessarily all bad. For example, consider what happens in the marketplace for a commodity like grains.

Suppose ranchers know they will need a supply of grain four months from now, but they can't be sure what the price will be then. The commodity might go sky high at that time, putting the profitability of their livestock business in jeopardy. This would happen if, for example, there is a poor harvest due to crop failure or a long dry spell. There would then be a decreased supply which means an increased demand and therefore higher prices. The rancher can offset this risk by buying a "futures contract." **A futures contract is the right**, **but not an obligation**, **to a specific amount of a commodity at a certain price in the future.** Note that the rancher doesn't contract to buy the grain itself—just the right to buy grain. This right is removed from the actual product itself i.e. the grain. This is an example of what is referred to as a product of the virtual market, i.e. a derivative.

This all becomes possible because of the existence of the speculators, who buy and sell future contracts with the expectation that by assuming risk they will make profits. Here it is clear that the speculators help to enhance business operations and the economy in general. They create liquidity and depth for the market.

But speculation is much less desirable when the derivative gets too far removed from the real commodity. That was the situation with many banks and investment firms that went overboard buying and selling risky, "hyper virtual" contracts for huge commissions. In the end these institutions ran up tremendous losses from virtual market speculation.

Back to emerging markets: economists assumed that development would inevitably entail growth of the virtual economy, just as it has happened in the West. But because of the innovative financing methods that work closely with the real economy, the emerging markets will avoid the unsustainable expansion of a virtual economy. While growing in this way, the Emerging economies will thus avoid the mushrooming of financial entities with their high fees that sap profits.

The second major miscalculation was the underestimation of domestic demand. As the emerging countries increased production, a new breed of consumers will materialize to drive a flurry of new products that will be made available by local producers. The demand for European exports will be zilch.

Obama—Kloppenberg incomplete

We have mentioned Kloppenberg's faulty assessment of Obama's intellectual formation, which failed to take into the Alinsky contribution—which would nullify any guarantee of truth in Obama's statements or writings. An additional deficit is that Obama, having fallen prey to the progressive re-narration of history, lacks an understanding of the foundations of Western Civilization. This has led him to underestimate of the American people's ability to commit to self-imposed austerity. Ignoring the legacy of the Hebraic-Greek underpinnings of the Western psyche, he measured the nation's conviction on a numerical scale, believing that his experience as an African American could outcompete a people he consistently labeled as "selfish," "lazy," and "flawed" when he was addressing international audiences. But not accepting the concept of transcendence, he failed to realize that the scale is not linear. When it comes to sacrificing to make things better for themselves and their children, the commitment scale includes octaves beyond his own comprehension.

In his inaugural address, John F. Kennedy acknowledged this tradition of the Western heritage of the American people:

> Let every nation know, whether it wishes us well or ill, that we shall pay any price, bear any burden, meet any hardship, support any friend, oppose any foe, in order to assure the survival and the success of liberty.

Americans will sacrifice with unrepatriation of profits while the progressive power based on the financial reserves dwindles.

The progressive government will, in the end, become a welfare state funded by an increasingly reluctant consortium of wealthy internationalists, who will eventually be as relieved to see it go as they were to see the end of the European Union.

CHAPTER 35

Cincinnatus Cometh

In 1963 paper in *World Politics,* Zbigniew Brzezinski begins his discussion on political leadership in modern society with a famous quote from Lenin: "Kto kovo?" asking "who governs?" Brzezinski's analysis lays out features of the governments of history and compares them to what's new in the current world.

There are the "whos";—that is, those that govern—and the "others," those that are influenced by the "whos." For "whos," think mainly of political leaders and government people in the public arena. This would be those who follow the path that politicians pursued through party affiliation (Durbanism), ascending to government leadership.

On the other hand, there are those who are nonpolitical and control government by way of wealth, income, or expertise. This would include those who are members of the Trilateral Commission, such as David Rockefeller and other banking principles, and, of course, George Soros, one of the world's wealthiest men.

A different response to crisis: Cincinnatus

Beyond this, however, from time to time, there opens up a new avenue of leadership, a new arena other than traditional law-making, and into this arena can emerge a new type of leader, one who in many ways reflects the qualities of a character from Roman History: Lucius Quinctius Cincinnatus. The Cincinnatus leadership type is the man or woman (Think Jeanne D'Arc), who emerges as a leader in the face of a crisis. Our scenario predicts a set of very likely crises on the horizon of 2020 America and points to very possible conditions in which a Cincinnatus could emerge.

The historical Cincinnatus was called on to serve Rome because of his outstanding leadership service to the greater good, as well as his civic virtue and modesty. He completed his task in defeating rival tribal enemies of the City of Rome. Once the task was done, he immediately resigned his absolute authority and returned to the plow from whence he came. In American history, a comparison has been made between Cincinnatus and George Washington. Once the crisis of the American Revolution had passed, Washington willingly gave up near absolute power. This contrasts with the rise in power of the American *apparatchik* and the principles of Durbanism.

By the year 2019, the American government will have suffered a severe loss of financial reserves due to a decline in GDP, entitlement payments to the *apparatchik*, and costly interest rate payments on considerable debts that have accrued during and prior to the Obama administration. In addition the losses from the backing of EU bailout plans further curtailed financial reserves indirectly The democratization of unrepatriation of profits as mentioned in the previous chapter is another unexpected problem.

The administration will have demonstrated its incompetency at every turn, from health care to border instability, and the growing power of organizations policing almost every aspect of daily life will have become a source of great resentment among the American public.

In addition, the ruling elite will have become unable to effectively communicate with the American people. As popular as they once were, presidential appearances will no longer be feasible due to a lack of attendance and the inability to provide for sufficient security. The systematic boycott of video presentations, which frequently end up becoming material for popular satire, render satellite messaging ineffective.

In attempting to quash the infringement on public liberties, the Supreme Court will have retaliated against the administration's unilateral declaration of law. Through a series of Writs of Certiorari fed into the court by way of appeal courts of cooperating states, the justices will have begun to issue rulings at unheard of speed, sometimes even daily. This dazzling display of jurisprudence will have the effect of preventing fines and imprisonment among the population.

But this interference will have prompted the administration to issue a ruling that the Supreme Court and other state courts cannot hear such cases until it has dealt with other materials before it. The justices, will decline to cooperate—some, like Alito, in order to prevent arrest and imprisonment—will attempt to make judgments in hiding. Justice Roberts, however, having refused to submit to advice from supporters to do likewise, will continue to make public appearances until the time of his arrest. Roberts was seized and forcefully disrobed in private.

Cincinnatus cometh

What are the key features of a Cincinnatus leadership? To begin with, he arises in the setting of some crisis. Unlike the progressive motivations, Cincinnatus docs not appear in order to exploit a crisis, but rather because he can offer an almost immediate solution. His control of the situation must be absolute, which means that he must have achieved a great deal of trust. Unlike the Obama progressive rule, which proceeds from planned divisiveness, the Cincinnatus control requires cohesion of the people he serves. Another essential characteristic is competence. He must be able to solve the problem and end the suffering in short order. Since he is not dependent on public financial support to begin with, he is able to return to his prior vocation, laying down all power.

In the matter of predicting the arenas in which the new leadership model of Cincinnatus will emerge, we consider two: labor representation and the southern border initiative.

SEIU death knell

An often viewed YouTube segment shows Andy Stern grinning and saying with some satisfaction, "Workers of the world unite; that's not just a slogan anymore."

Indeed, it's not. Is it death knell for the SEIU.

As the service employees union expands overseas, it will align itself with the various foreign governments just as it did in the United States. But as the governments fall, so do the easily identified unions. In Third-World countries a financial crisis can quickly accelerate out of control compared to the US. The greed that SEIU manifests in the United States will be exponentially magnified under such circumstances along with the visibility of the organization's lack of rank-and-file leadership. The cause that a Cincinnatus-like character will adopt will be the same as it was in the solidarity movement led by Lech Wałęsa in the Gdańsk Shipyard—it will be a demand for bread. The overseas crisis will begin to accelerate the unraveling, which has already started in the States.

As already mentioned, a feature of the American entity in the later part of Obama Two will be increasing regionalization due to increasing power of individual states, and this will bring unprecedented support to reformers of SEIU, such as Maya Morris who spoke out in 2008 SEIU meeting in San Juan, Puerto Rico. Separated from their national strength, the SEIU *apparatchik* will face increasing demands for representation by rank-and-file members.

The second, and probably more important, Cincinnatus arena will involve the states of the Southern Border.

A battle in New Mexico?

The predicted crisis here will take place about 2019. It will begin with an Illinois-based movement by Hispanic parents demanding that members of school boards in the districts where their children are educated be decided by open public elections. Support for the democratic measure will come from a growing antiprogressive collective, based primarily in states of the Southern Border mainly Texas, New Mexico, and Arizona. Support will come from a number of northern states as well.

The progressive administration attacked the parent-driven measure, declaring it in violation of the entrenched health care directives and the Law for Fairness in Education directives that passed in 2016. These directives required that both the nomination of candidates for all school board members and their subsequent approval must be provided by the Fairness Counsels, which are part of the new Obama militia. Furthermore, the administration ordered that all school boards nationwide immediately comply with the progressive ruling.

Notice was given by the Obama administration to the southern border states that appeared to have united against the federal ruling. But rather than proceed with passive resistance, which has been their usual response to federal rulings, the collective governorship of the southern states made it clear they would not comply.

Obama out of it

Before the confrontation between the southern states and the federal government begins, the scenario predicts that Obama will have personally withdrawn from any position in the government. As unlikely as that sounds to some, it is really not all that unbelievable considering his past. Obama has never stayed very long at any particular job. It has become apparent that as president of the United States he seems most attracted by the opportunity for lots of breaks with abundant time for recreation and travel.

Then, too, being the most powerful individual in the world first as president and then dictator can get a bit boring for someone like Obama.

Take the Nobel Peace Prize thing for example. The first time is really great, but it loses something of its edge the second time around. There's all that required dressing up in yesteryear's fashions, and, if it's not the same dull, old faces and strained smiles you had to put up with last time, then it's a new crop of equally dull, equally old faces and strained smiles. Then, too, the weather in Sweden may appear much less desirable than in other locations, such as Hawaii.

While Michelle Obama will likely remain First Lady until the end of progressive rule, in effect Obama himself will have little to do with the office as President by 2019. What will he do instead? He is attracted to the entertainment industry, manifesting his ability to sing and he has already submitted a screenplay to a Hollywood producer. (It was rejected.) He may even turn to a career in science.

The secret southern states conference and Mexico

The administration began measures to enforce the provisions of the Education Act by means of federal troops, but the administration was unaware of a second movement that had taken place.

Prior to the development of the education crisis, leaders of the states of Arizona, New Mexico, Texas, and certain townships in California, in violation of the US Constitution, entered into a series of meetings and negotiations with selected members of the Mexican government in order to achieve security and end the violence of the drug cartels.

A new government plan would involve changes for both Mexico and the United States. Mexico would be divided into four, more or less, autonomous states. These would include Baja on the Western border and Mexico Nord, or North Mexico, with a border contiguous with the American states. The other

Mexican states would include Guadelupe in the central portion and Panamaya in the South. Certain administrative functions would be retained in the capital, Mexico City.

In addition to the creation of Mexican states, the US border states would enter into an agreement with Mexico Nord. This would provide for the elimination of a border between North Mexico and the United States and the extermination of the drug cartel. In addition, the approval by both North Mexican citizens and citizens of the US southern states would be required for the passage of certain laws.

In the Spring of 2019, our scenario forecasts a confrontation, most likely in New Mexico, where we predict two US Marine divisions and a task force from the Second Infantry would arrive to carry out the government mandate of enforcing educational control. Mass defections of both leadership and troops from the federal forces will be followed by negotiations between the southern governments and the federal military.

The failure to enforce mandated educational measures will eventually lead to the collapse of the Washington-based federal government. Several progressive leaders will commit suicide. The use of federal troops to assist in the clearing of the cartels will end most of the border violence between Mexico and the United States.

Sometime before the fall of 2020, a state, probably Rhode Island, will propose a national referendum to restore representative government. Elections will likely take place a month after the referendum's acceptance by the nation.

Why did Obama's progressive regime fail?

James V. Schall relates an answer that then Cardinal Ratzinger (now Pope Benedict XVI) gave to the question: "Why does faith still have a chance?" The future pope replied, "Because it is in harmony with what man is…In man there is an inextinguishable yearning for the infinite."

We can draw from this conversation a parallel: Why is it always possible to overcome totalitarian progressive rule? In the end, progressivism, for all its claims at advancement, is an adventure in the pursuit of insufficient answers and unfulfillment of human needs.

Appendix:

A. Jaffee Memorandum.

B. Timeline of Forecasted Events.

C. Glossary of Isms and other such terms.

Memorandum to Bernard Berelson (President, Population Council) found in "Activities Relevant to the Study of Population Policy for the U.S." 3/11/69 by Frederick S. Jaffe (Vice-president of Planned Parenthood - World Population).

TABLE 1. Examples of Proposed Measures to Reduce U.S. Fertility, by Universality or Selectivity of Impact

Universal Impact	Selective Impact Depending on Socio-Economic Status	Measures Predicated on Existing Motivation to Prevent Unwanted Pregnancies
Social Constraints	Economic Deterrents	Social Controls
Restructure family: a) Postpone or avoid marriage b) Alter image of ideal family size	Modify tax policies: a) Substantial marriage tax b) Child Tax c) Tax married more than single d) Remove parents tax exemption d) Additional taxes on parents with more than 1 or 2 children in school	Compulsory abortion of out-of-wedlock pregnancies
Compulsory education of children	Reduce/eliminate paid maternity leave or benefits	Compulsory sterilization of all who have two children except for a few who would be allowed three
Encourage increased homosexuality	Reduce/eliminate children's or family allowances	Confine childbearing to only a limited number of adults
Educate for family limitation	Bonuses for delayed marriage and greater child-spacing	Stock certificate type permits for children
Fertility control agents in water supply	Pensions for women of 45 with less than N children	Housing Policies: a) Discouragement of private home ownership b) Stop awarding public housing based on family size
Encourage women to work	Eliminate Welfare payemnts after first 2 children	
	Chronic Depression	
	Require women to work and provide few child care facilities	
	Limit/eliminate public-financed medical care, scholarships, housing, loans and subsidies to families with more than N children.	

Measures Predicated on Existing Motivation to Prevent Unwanted Pregnancies:
- Payments to encourage sterilization
- Payments to encourage contraception
- Payments to encourage abortion
- Abortion and sterilization on demand
- Allow certain contraceptives to be distributed non-medically
- Improve contraceptive technology
- Make contraception truly available and accessible to all
- Improve maternal health care, with family planning a core element

Source: "A Family Planning Perspectives Special Supplement" published by Planned Parenthood-World Population, NYC, NY, 19.70.

267

Timeline for *The Next 2000 Days*.

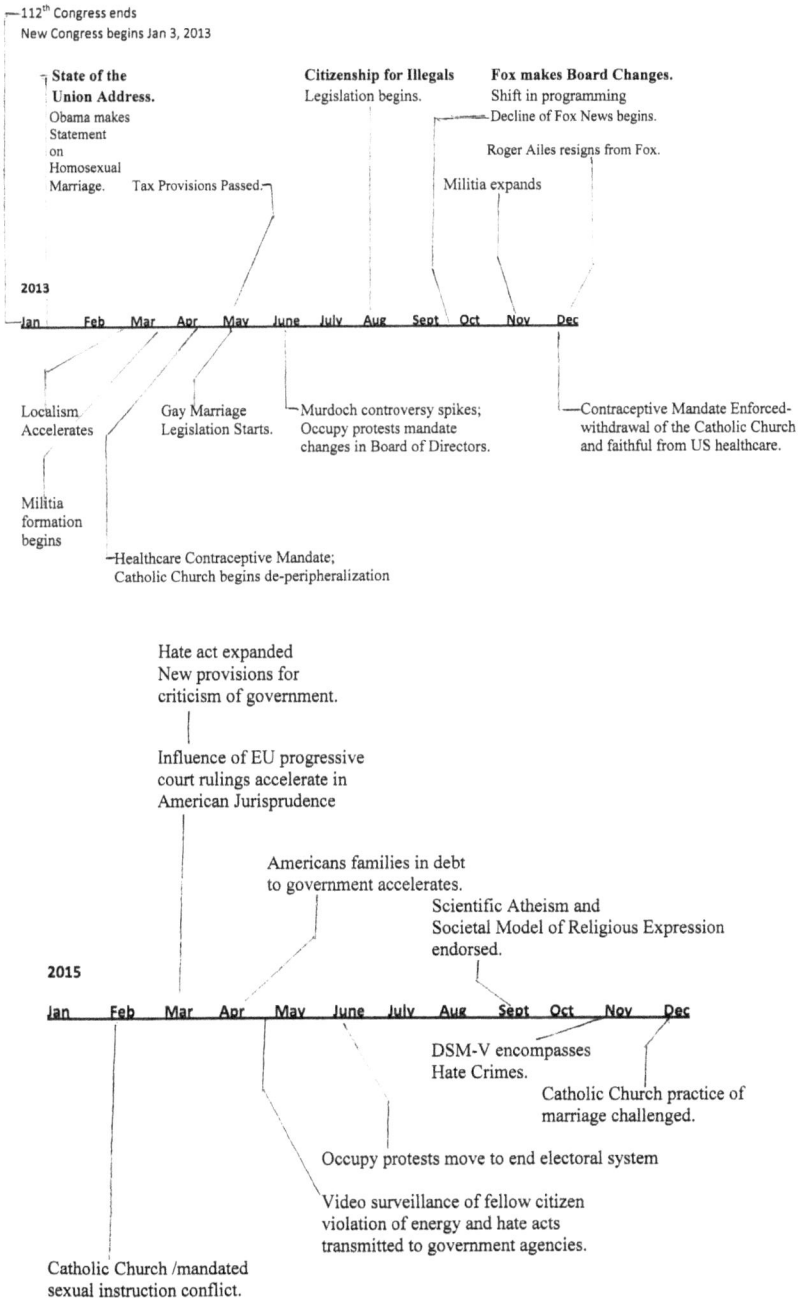

—112th Congress ends
New Congress begins Jan 3, 2013

State of the
Union Address.
Obama makes
Statement
on
Homosexual
Marriage.   Tax Provisions Passed.

Citizenship for Illegals
Legislation begins.

Fox makes Board Changes.
Shift in programming
—Decline of Fox News begins.

Roger Ailes resigns from Fox.

Militia expands

2013

Jan   Feb   Mar   Apr   May   June   July   Aug   Sept   Oct   Nov   Dec

Localism.
Accelerates

Gay Marriage
Legislation Starts.

—Murdoch controversy spikes;
Occupy protests mandate
changes in Board of Directors.

—Contraceptive Mandate Enforced-
withdrawal of the Catholic Church
and faithful from US healthcare.

Militia
formation
begins

—Healthcare Contraceptive Mandate;
Catholic Church begins de-peripheralization

Hate act expanded
New provisions for
criticism of government.

Influence of EU progressive
court rulings accelerate in
American Jurisprudence

Americans families in debt
to government accelerates.

Scientific Atheism and
Societal Model of Religious Expression
endorsed.

2015

Jan   Feb   Mar   Apr   May   June   July   Aug   Sept   Oct   Nov   Dec

DSM-V encompasses
Hate Crimes.

Catholic Church practice of
marriage challenged.

Occupy protests move to end electoral system

Video surveillance of fellow citizen
violation of energy and hate acts
transmitted to government agencies.

Catholic Church /mandated
sexual instruction conflict.

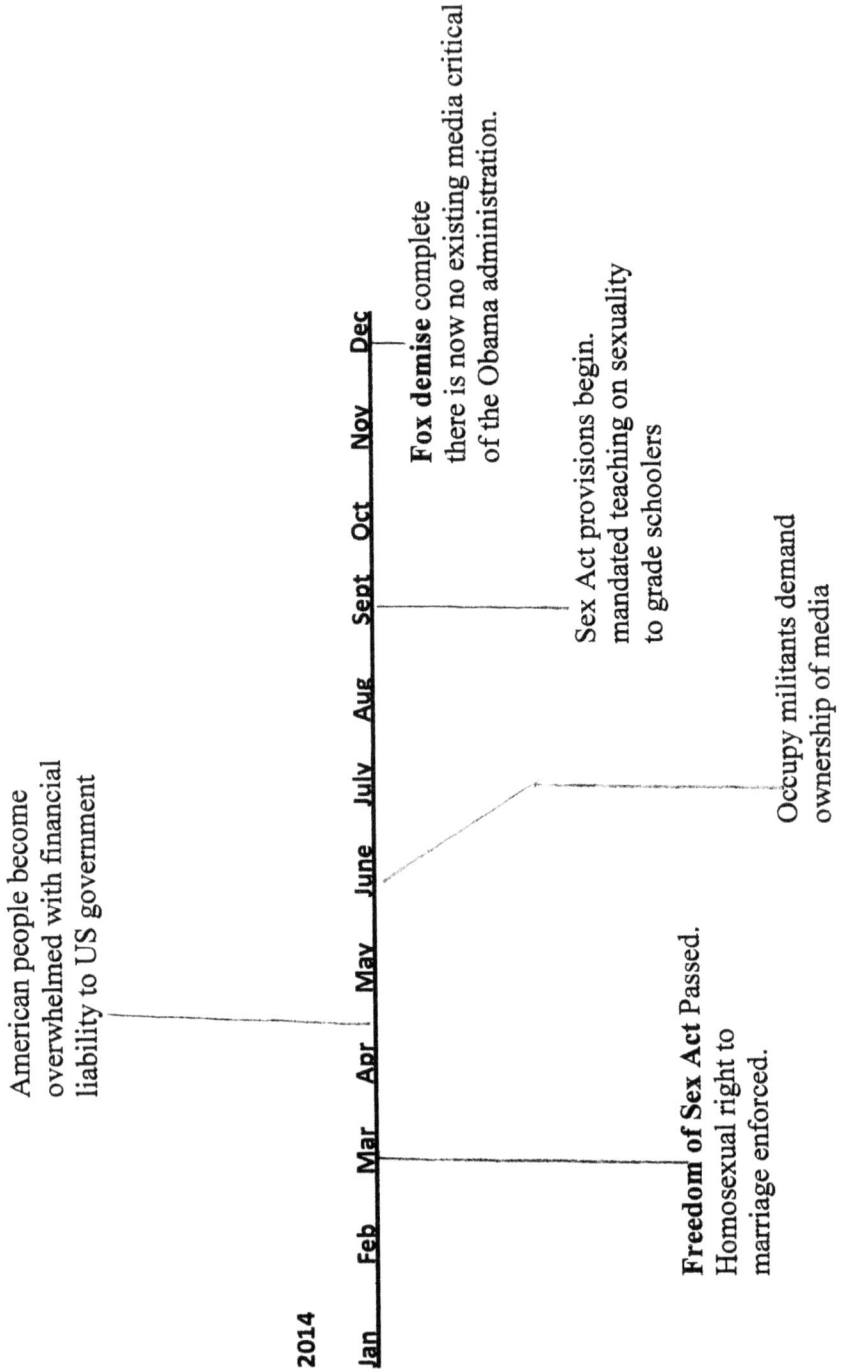

American people become
overwhelmed with financial
liability to US government

Fox demise complete
there is now no existing media critical
of the Obama administration.

Dec
Nov
Oct
Sept

Sex Act provisions begin.
mandated teaching on sexuality
to grade schoolers

Aug
July
June
May

Occupy militants demand
ownership of media

Apr
Mar

Freedom of Sex Act Passed.
Homosexual right to
marriage enforced.

Feb
Jan

2014

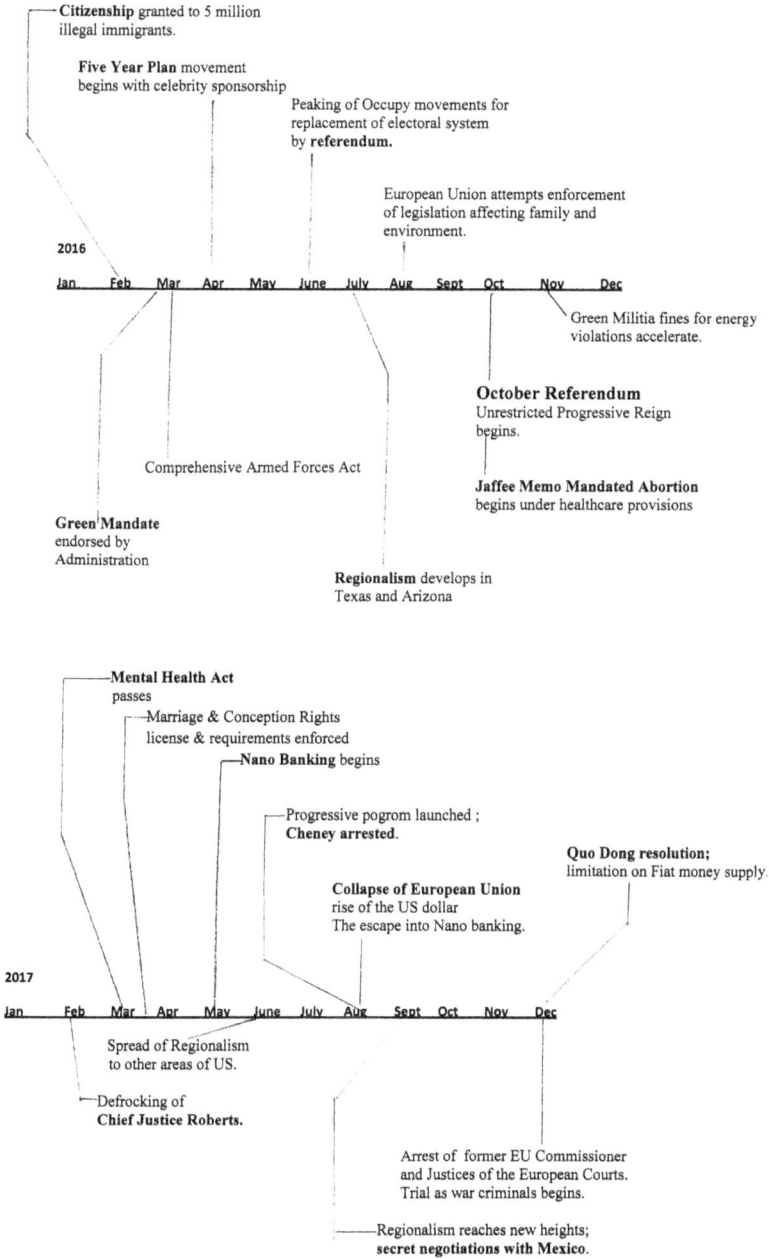

Citizenship granted to 5 million
illegal immigrants.

Five Year Plan movement
begins with celebrity sponsorship

Peaking of Occupy movements for
replacement of electoral system
by **referendum.**

European Union attempts enforcement
of legislation affecting family and
environment.

2016

| Jan. | Feb | Mar | Apr | May | June | July | Aug | Sept | Oct | Nov | Dec |

Green Militia fines for energy
violations accelerate.

October Referendum
Unrestricted Progressive Reign
begins.

Comprehensive Armed Forces Act

Jaffee Memo Mandated Abortion
begins under healthcare provisions

Green Mandate
endorsed by
Administration

Regionalism develops in
Texas and Arizona

Mental Health Act
passes

Marriage & Conception Rights
license & requirements enforced

Nano Banking begins

Progressive pogrom launched ;
Cheney arrested.

Quo Dong resolution;
limitation on Fiat money supply.

Collapse of European Union
rise of the US dollar
The escape into Nano banking.

2017

| Jan. | Feb | Mar | Apr | May | June | July | Aug | Sept | Oct | Nov | Dec |

Spread of Regionalism
to other areas of US.

Defrocking of
Chief Justice Roberts.

Arrest of former EU Commissioner
and Justices of the European Courts.
Trial as war criminals begins.

Regionalism reaches new heights;
secret negotiations with Mexico.

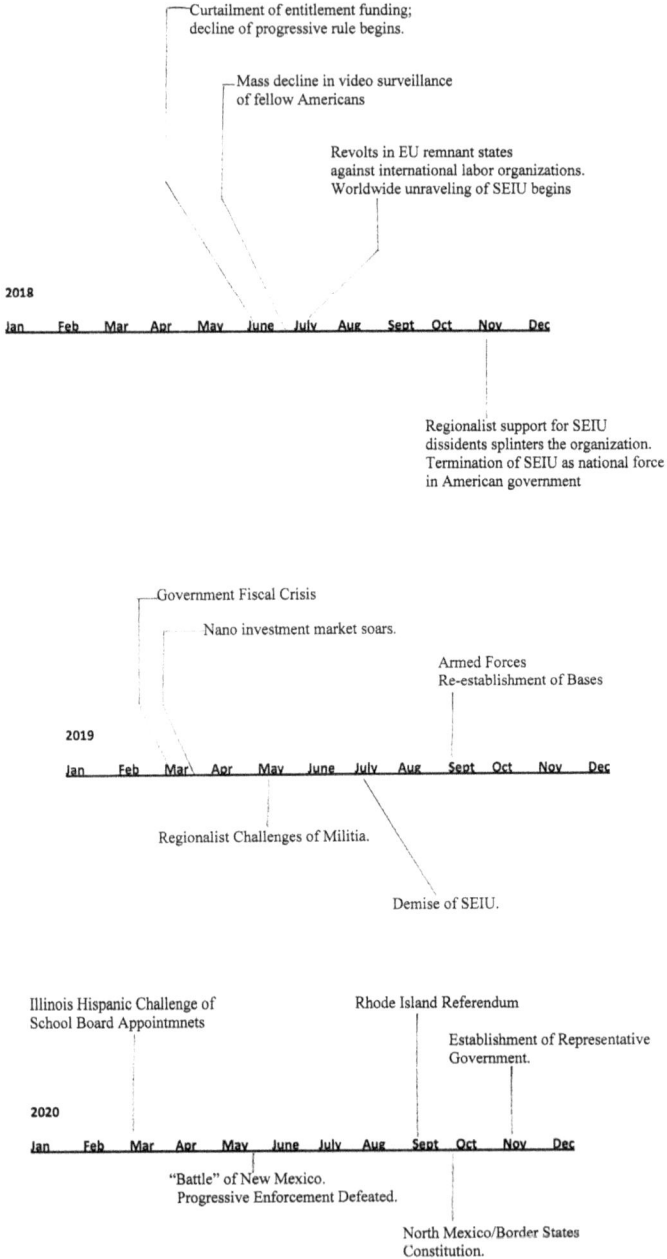

Curtailment of entitlement funding;
decline of progressive rule begins.

Mass decline in video surveillance
of fellow Americans

Revolts in EU remnant states
against international labor organizations.
Worldwide unraveling of SEIU begins

2018

Jan   Feb   Mar   Apr   May   June   July   Aug   Sept   Oct   Nov   Dec

Regionalist support for SEIU
dissidents splinters the organization.
Termination of SEIU as national force
in American government

Government Fiscal Crisis

Nano investment market soars.

Armed Forces
Re-establishment of Bases

2019

Jan   Feb   Mar   Apr   May   June   July   Aug   Sept   Oct   Nov   Dec

Regionalist Challenges of Militia.

Demise of SEIU.

Illinois Hispanic Challenge of
School Board Appointmnets

Rhode Island Referendum

Establishment of Representative
Government.

2020

Jan   Feb   Mar   Apr   May   June   July   Aug   Sept   Oct   Nov   Dec

"Battle" of New Mexico.
Progressive Enforcement Defeated.

North Mexico/Border States
Constitution.

Adlerianism. Based on Adler's Theory that humans develop from a natural state of inferiority to superiority. Emphasizes the profound social significance of individual acts of sexuality.

Alinsky. Saul Alinsky, author of *Rules for Radicals,* a text used by Obama and dedicated to Satan.

Axelrodianism. David Axelrod formulated "Fox is not a news organization" and demonstrated the Alinsky principle of diversion of issue in argumentation. He did not charge Fox with making a libelous statement; rather, Axelrod launched the debate about whether it was a news organization at all. This ploy also used the Lenin Corollary: Eliminate Fox New and you eliminate criticism. Eliminate criticism and you eliminate the introduction of outside agendas.

Billings Ovulation Method. An alternative method of birth control—often confused with the ineffective rhythm method—as effective as oral contraceptive and compatible with the teaching of Roman Catholic Church. For more information, see http://www.thebillingsovulationmethod.org/.

Chuttism. Refers to the principle derived from the teaching of Ryan Chittum who declared that those who inform themselves of the content of Murdoch media (by reading publications, for example) share the guilt for crimes committed by Murdoch.

Freudian. In the scenario we use Freudian as a contrast to Adlerian, both representations of human behavior. The Freudian approach looks for deep-seated pathological expressions in human behavior. Adlerian analysis looks at ways to develop naturally to a more superior state. The Freudian perspective dominates American society.

Hegelian. Refers to a viewpoint of history based on the influential theory of Georg Wilhelm Friedrich Hegel (1770–1831) in which an element of violence is the necessary requisite for advancing society.

Jenkinsianism. Based on the behavior of John Jenkins, the president of University of Notre Dame, a putative Catholic university. Mr. Jenkins provided the first step of the pragmatic advance of Obama's Alinsky approach to youth. The approach begins by insisting there is the possibility of an underlying agreement between the progressive agenda and religion, encouraging a "meeting of the minds." Then later, the progressives assure youth that the agreement can only be obtained through a pragmatic understanding of the limitation of the validity of religion. Jenkinsianism disguises the intentions of the progressives. That intention is not only to remain closed to discourse of any kind, but also to espouse the agenda to destroy any obstacle to audience acceptance of progressivism (which usually means promoting the abandoning one's religious faith).

Inverse Lenin Corollary. This states that the introduction of a new agenda implies criticism. This is a simple inversion of Lenin's Corollary and has been applied by the Catholic hierarchy in regard to human husbandry.

Kloppenberg Incomplete. The inability of academia to pursue truth in analysis of progressive politics. Analysis of Obama, whose espousal of the Alinsky philosophy compromises the truth of his statements, is an excellent example of this. The loss of perception of truth demonstrates the widespread degeneration of once scholarly educational establishments, as documented by William Buckley in his famous 1950s review of Yale University.

Lenin Corollary. Based on the opening of Lenin's "Who Rules?" wherein Lenin notes that criticism of any kind brings the risk of entering a new agenda.

Losses. Also referred to as "The Four Great Losses of Freedom." and the associated isms.

They are the loss of Freedom of "say"—Axelrodianism

Freedom of "read"—Chuttism

Freedom of "think"—Matthewism

Freedom of "be"—Obamanism

Matthewism. The incessant need to assign preformulated progressive-agenda-detracting motives to anyone opposing a certain view point. This is reflected in well-known MSNBC progressive Kevin Matthews, who consistently ascribes any criticism of Obama to racism, either overt or deep seated.

Obamanism. The loss of an individual's freedom to live when such a life is in opposition to the progressive agenda. This is manifested in his willingness to destroy the life of an infant that manages to survive an abortion attempt. The concept extends to the support of anti-life measures of contraception, mandated abortion, and the progressive pogrom that, according to our scenario, will result in arrest, torture, and execution of those in opposition to progressive rule.

Pragmatism. -This is a difficult term to define. We have formulated it from William James in a way that best allows understanding of Progressivism.

Progressivism.

Progressive is an adjective used here to apply to political movements. I have been frequently asked precisely what I mean by the term progressive especially since one looks at the ease with which I identified the Obama progressive rule with that of the horrific Third Reich and the Stalinist Terror. Is *progressive* then something intrinsically evil? Certainly not! A distinction should be made between the use of *progressive* to describe certain political entities and the more general meaning of the term, which may in fact refer to a good thing. In reality little happens in the world without a progressive outlook. The progressive spirit is easily identified in Christianity with the gospel imperative to go forth and change the world.

The problem starts when the progressive spirit is distorted. This occurs when the leaders of progressive political movements place agenda about the dignity and destiny of man as a spiritual being, denying his call to a divine destiny.

That almost always occurs when the characteristic expression of progressive rule is associated with pragmatic restrictions on religion.

The progressive regime will, in the end, collide with established religion, especially the Catholic Church, although it is frequently the members of other Christian churches that are the first to courageously speak out. Progressives are quick to reply that the churches are merely looking out for their own interests. Nonetheless, history documents that both the hierarchy and the faithful consistently manifest the willingness to suffer all things in order to bear witness to progressive regime violation of mankind.

When full-blown, the progressive rule will turn on the progeny of humankind, starting with the "weeds" of society. To this end Margaret Sanger, founder of Planned Parenthood, offered a program that was paralleled by the Nazi terror that enveloped Europe, in which the "weeds" in need of extermination were the mentally and physically disabled, Jews, Gypsies, and homosexuals.

Many point with pride to Obama, a strong supporter of Planned Parenthood, the first black man in the White House. Many have told me how they wished their parents could have lived to see this event. But in the progressive scheme of things, given their longstanding quest for power, the man in the White House is merely a gimmick to allow what will almost assuredly come later. Obama is like a talisman hoisted on high with the proclamation, "Forsake this and you shall forever be in constant retreat from historical destiny." Unfortunately, the destiny that follows will come as a shock to many Americans.

***Quo Dong* Resolution.** A definitive December 2017 notice issued by the Central Bank of China to the US government informing them that any attempts to print new money would result in large-scale flooding of the international markets with US debt securities.

Real Katolique.-The name used to refers to an increasing group of individuals that refer to themselves as Catholics but are actually in discord with orthodox teachings of the Roman Church. They have been growing in number especially since Vatican II and the issuance of the encyclical "Humanae Vitae."

They assume leadership positions in both secular and parish administration and direct much of the social activities of both areas. Their movement is met with muted Vatican resistance at this point in time.

www.ingramcontent.com/pod-product-compliance
Lightning Source LLC
LaVergne TN
LVHW051457080426
835509LV00017B/1797